Expert 21st Century Advice on

SELLING YOUR HOME FOR

MAXIMUM PROFIT

DAVID HARRELL

EXPERT 21ˢᵗ CENTURY ADVICE on
SELLING YOUR HOME for MAXIMUM PROFIT

Published by BriteRock Investment Group, LLC
101 Stone Block Row, Ste 661, Montchanin, DE 19710

Cover design by Holly Feldheim

First Edition: 2020
Library of Congress Control Number: 2020904715
ISBN 978-1-7347482-0-8 (pbk); ISBN 978-1-7347482-1-5 (ebk)
Manufactured in the United States of America

Dedication

This book is dedicated to my wife Edris along with the rest of my loving family. Thank you for making my journey so joyous and meaningful.

TABLE OF CONTENTS

Introduction

If you are like most people, your home is your number one asset, containing precious equity you'd like to take with you. This book is written to give you firsthand knowledge of how to best sell your home and retain as much equity as possible. It doesn't matter if you plan to sell the home yourself or utilize a real estate agent, this book will guide you on your journey no matter which path you choose to follow.

In this book you will get a 22+ year real estate education in just a few hours of reading and will learn valuable lessons from the mistakes I made early on in the business. Once completed, you will have obtained a bachelor's degree in real estate sales, along with a minor in *Real Estate School of Hard Knocks*. This is a must-read for anyone interested in learning as much as they can about the selling process from an insider's point of view.

You will also read excerpts from other related professionals in the field of accounting, real estate law, home inspection services, mortgage lending, interior design and staging, along with other experts sharing their knowledge and inside tips about selling your home for maximum profit.

Since you will most likely also be purchasing another property, this book also contains relevant buyer information to assist you with your purchase.

This is an easy to read, down to earth book that is to the point and chock full of professional advice you won't read in other books. It also includes real life examples along with hypothetical case studies for easy to understand scenarios which allow readers to experience problem situations firsthand.

To keep things simple, I provide you with useful **TIP's** and **NOTE's** containing insightful advice in each chapter. You will also find a handy Glossary at the end of the book. Feel free to reference it anytime you are unsure of a particular term, as this will provide you with a better understanding of the real estate jargon so you're not perceived as an amateur when talking with other real estate professionals.

Lastly, there are four handy checklists in the appendix, including:

- For-Sale Checklist
- Open House Checklist
- Closing Checklist
- Moving Timeline Checklist

Grab a cool drink along with a notepad and pen. Relax in your most comfortable chair, kick off your shoes and let's get started!

Real Estate Dave

PART I:

GETTING STARTED

Chapter 1

Home Work

"Knowledge is Power."
~Sir Francis Bacon

You've lived in your home for a long time and you now realize that your house is too big, too small, not close enough to family or too far to commute to your job, etc. Perhaps you and your significant other are suddenly empty nesters because the kids have moved out and the house is now just too quiet. Whatever the reason, you want out and the timing is right, since it just doesn't make sense to live there anymore.

Now what? How do you take the initial step into getting it in gear?

First off, you need to know where you want to go and how you want to live. Are you ready for the condo lifestyle where someone else takes care of the lawn and garden, fixes the roof, and deals with the many other chores involved with homeownership? Or are you just ready for a smaller home, with less to clean, not as much maintenance and fewer utility expenses? Perhaps a newer ranch home would satisfy all of your needs in your next house.

Maybe you want all of the above, along with your meals taken care of so you no longer have to cook. Retirement communities can be all-inclusive, with fitness centers, health facilities, auditoriums for movies, plays, concerts and other forms of entertainment. If this is more your speed, you will want to start exploring the area in which you want to live in order to find out how much it will cost you per month.

NOTE: *Retirement communities can be ridiculously expensive, anywhere from $5,000 to $10,000 per month. Yes, per month! Staggering, isn't it? It's most likely even higher in large metropolitan cities such as New York, San Francisco, Chicago, etc.*

It's important to know where you are headed and how much it will cost, because you need to know if it's going to be doable after you sell your home. For example, if the sale of your home nets you $325,000 and you want to go into a retirement home that costs $8,000 per month, or $96,000 per year, that only gives you a little over three years' worth of living expenses not including any retirement income and it could leave you in a crunch. The last thing you want to do is be forced to get a part-time job to pay for your living expenses. Now, there is nothing wrong with a part-time job if you want one. In fact, I plan to work well into my retirement. However, it's one thing to want to work and it's quite the other to HAVE to work. Big difference, so plan accordingly.

<u>Geographic Research</u>

If you think you may want to move out of state and would like to gather some good information on other areas of the country, I recommend the book *Places Rated Almanac,* by David Savageau. It is chock full of data, including weather, cost-of-living expenses, population statistics and lots of other relevant data. My wife and I used this book when we decided we wanted a change from the mid-Atlantic. We studied the book extensively and visited many of the places that looked attractive to us, such as Arizona, New Mexico and North Carolina. Ironically, at the end of the day we stayed put, because we realized we preferred to be near our families. Although we didn't move out of state, we found the book to be a valuable tool in learning all about other areas in the U.S.A. They have many different editions now, such as a retirement edition, etc.

Nerdwallet.com and *payscale.com* each have a free comparison tool where you can plug in your total annual income along with your current address and input where you are interested in moving. It will tell you if you will need to be making more or less money in order to maintain your current standard of living. You don't want to go to all the trouble of moving only to find out that your current income is not going to be sufficient in your area.

It's also important to know if you will be able to purchase your next property before you sell your current property. If not, you will need to make your purchase *contingent upon the sale of your current residence.* This can be a real tightrope act deserving of some serious consideration. Because of this, I've devoted an entire chapter to it (see Chapter 3). It's important you know the complexities of buying and selling at the same time.

In the next chapter, I will review the best time of year to sell your number one investment. It's important if possible that you time it right so you are exposed to the greatest number of buyers competing for your home.

Chapter 2

Best Time to Sell

"Observe due measure, for right timing is in all things the most important factor."
~Hesiod, Greek poet

Everyone's situation is different and not everyone can sell at the most opportune time. Job changes, divorce, illness and death are just some uncontrollable factors that may determine when you will need to sell your home.

Rest assured, there is ALWAYS a market to peddle your abode, no matter what month it is. Buyers also have many of the same circumstances, compelling them to move at different times of the year.

In my opinion, the absolute best time to sell a property is between April and June. Those three months are by far the hottest months in which to sell a home. One big reason for this is because families with children want to move when the kids will be on summer break to make it easier on the family. I suspect much of the country has a similar peak season for those very same reasons.

How Weather Can Affect You

However, as with many rules, there are exceptions. The one big exception in real estate is the weather. If March turns out to be mild with warmer temperatures and not a lot of precipitation, then the market could easily heat up one month early. When I sell a property, I am ready to go in March but will wait and see how the weather presents itself and *play it by ear.*

If, on the other hand, March is cold and bitter and April is cool with consistent rain, the market may get off to a slow start and might very well not get going until May, which in turn may extend the selling market into July or August. There is no telling what the forecast is going to be, so my advice to you is to be ready, just in case we have an early spring.

There are advantages and disadvantages to marketing your home during the peak season. The obvious advantage is there are lots of buyers looking for properties. With the added buyers comes a very good chance that you will be able to snag one and sell for maximum value. One of the conundrums buyers face when shopping during the peak season is the fear of losing out on a property. Because they realize there is so much competition, as evidenced by bustling open houses and overlapping showings, buyers may feel under the gun to make quick decisions because they are afraid of losing out on a property they like.

This puts purchasers in a quagmire, because although they may like a property, though perhaps not love it, they realize it may be the best house they will be able to find in their price range, so they feel compelled to put in an offer for fear of losing out to someone else. I see this most often with buyers that have lost out on one or two prior homes where they were not the winning bidders and thus lost the house to another purchaser. Once a buyer loses a house or two to the competition, it spurs them on to put their best foot forward and ensure this does not happen on the next property they like. It's a wonderful phenomenon for sellers, because it means their home has a great chance of selling for a very good price. If it weren't for the competition, buyers would feel more at ease, knowing they have a little more time to decide if a house really is right for them.

Peak Season

Thus, the peak market is a boon for sellers due to the high demand and limited inventory. It's similar to the game musical chairs we played when we were kids. No one wants to be the one left without a chair or a house.

Recent economic conditions, such as aging baby boomers deciding to stay put for a while, corporations not relocating employees as often as they used to and current owners not feeling compelled to move up into bigger homes has created a housing shortage. Simple economics of supply and demand dictates that when demand is high and supply is limited, prices rise due to increased competition. Another big win for sellers.

Sellers can truly benefit if they are one of the first homes into the peak season, since there are usually a bunch of buyers ready and waiting, some of whom may have lost out during the prior season. If March brings warmth and sunshine and you are early putting your *For-Sale* sign on the lawn, the real estate gods will be positioned in your favor.

The only downside to selling during the peak season is that there are many more homes for sale, and you will be facing some stiff competition, which makes it important to have your house looking its best so you can partake in the feeding frenzy of a peak market.

It's important to note that the seasonality of the market varies from location to location. Selling activity in the Midwest and Northeast gets much busier in the peak season than in any other region in the United States. Consequently, sales activity in the South and West are less impacted by the peak season where sales in the winter months are steadier.

Talk with local real estate agents to find out when your area marketplace is at its best. Then try and time it so you get to take advantage of the peak season. It is by far the best time to sell your most important asset.

In the next chapter, I will review real estate's *Catch 22*, and how it can negatively impact your deal. It's best to put some thought into this conceivable dilemma, so let's get started!

Chapter 3

Real Estate *Catch 22*

"Every exit is an entry somewhere."
~Tom Stoppard

So, by now you've done your homework and you know where you want to live and approximately how much it will cost to get into your new place. Before you make any firm commitments, it's time to put your current home under the microscope to see how you can maximize your profits to help you in your next adventure.

Home Sale Contingencies

The biggest *Catch 22* in real estate is the home sale contingency. Simply put, the purchase of your next property is contingent upon the sale of your existing property, meaning you need the proceeds from your current home in order to obtain financing and enable you to purchase your subsequent property. Of course, if you have enough equity in your current home, you can always borrow on it to purchase your next place. Many people don't have that luxury and still require a loan for their subsequent property. Hence the *Catch 22*. If this situation does not apply to you, move on to the next chapter. However, you will still learn some valuable ideas should the buyer of your current home make their purchase contingent upon the sale of their existing home.

It is important that you look into this situation now, because it can affect how you proceed with the sale of your home. For example, if you do require a home sale contingency on the purchase of your next property, it is a good idea to make the sale of your current home, *Sale contingent upon sellers finding a suitable home to purchase.* Right now you're probably thinking, what buyer is going to want to commit themselves to this kind of situation, knowing their purchase may take longer? That is a valid question, as some buyers will not consider it and will continue to keep looking.

The short answer is that most buyers will contemplate it if they really like your home and are in a position to ride out some time delays in order to purchase the property they adore. Examples of this are renters who are currently on a month to month rental contract with their landlord and can wait awhile for the house to close. They just continue renting until they hear things are looking better and then give notice of their departure to the landlord at the appropriate time. Another example would be a buyer living with their parents, or relatives until the deal is closed. I have encountered both scenarios and they've worked out perfectly.

Home sale contingencies can sometimes create a domino effect involving several houses all depending upon a prior home sale, which can be a very stressful situation with communications vital between the parties, so everyone knows what's going on. It is especially taxing on closing day when you have moving trucks for the buyer and seller scheduled and with timelines to meet. I don't recommend closing on two homes the same day as it is very nerve-wracking and stressful. It's tough on all parties including the real estate agents.

For example, Home A is to be sold on January 2nd but is contingent upon Home B's closing the same day. Home C is also scheduled to close on January 2nd and is contingent upon Home A's closing on the same day. Since all of the closings are dependent on each other, it's easy to see how one botched settlement can negatively affect the other two. Thus, the fear of contingency contracts.

I remember one closing in particular where the seller's moving company was moving boxes out of the home, while the purchaser's moving company was moving boxes inside the home. Both parties were worried their boxes would end up in the wrong place and rightfully so, especially since the seller was moving out of state. Technically the seller's contents are supposed to be out of the home at closing time, but the sellers did not notify anyone of this snafu. Thankfully, the buyers were very understanding and did not have a problem with it.

Should you find yourself needing to sell before purchasing, it is vitally important that your home be in tip-top condition and looking great so that a buyer will want to even consider purchasing your home with an uncertain closing date. Remember, the buyers may not be able to lock in their interest rate without a definitive settlement date. If they can lock in the rate, then the clock will be ticking down on when the rate expires, either within 30 to 60 days. Buyers will most likely have to pay additional fees if they wish to keep the interest rate locked in place. These out of pocket expenses can tarnish those warm and fuzzy feelings purchasers have about your home. Even more reason to ensure that it looks fantastic and worth the wait.

If things are delayed longer than anticipated, you may want to sweeten the deal and inform the buyers that you will be leaving your large screen mounted TV as an added inclusion. No, you certainly don't have to, but a happy buyer is more apt to close than an unhappy buyer. See Chapter 19 for more great inclusion incentives.

If you do fall under the real estate *Catch 22*, I suggest you look into other options for purchasing your home. For example, when we purchased our current home without a home sale contingency on our former home, I borrowed funds from my individual retirement account (IRA) to make the sale happen. I then replaced the funds when my prior home closed and it freed up the equity to pay back the IRA. Be sure to speak with your accountant, bank, or financial advisor about creative ideas for purchasing a home without a contingency clause.

Purchase Disadvantages

A big disadvantage of having to sell before you purchase is you are much more likely to pay a higher purchase price because of the home sale contingency. Many sellers don't want to take on the added risk, so they want a premium price, much like a lender requires higher interest rates for higher-risk buyers. You will also have a harder time purchasing newer listings, since many listing agents will advise against home sale contingencies, especially in the first few weeks of putting a house on the market, even more of a reason to get creative and purchase without the contingency.

I have heard buyers and sellers say they don't want to own two homes at the same time due to two mortgage payments, and so they choose to request the contingency. I completely understand that. However, if the homes are priced right and in good, saleable condition, then it should not pose a problem. Many of these same buyers and sellers have never purchased and sold on the same day and have no idea how incredibly stressful it can be, especially when you consider utility transfers, changing mailing addresses, moving trucks, attending two closings, etc., all at the same time.

TIP: *Homeowners insurance may not cover your losses if your home has been vacant for more than 30 days and you did not divulge this ahead of time. Be sure to discuss this with your insurance provider before vacating your property.*

Jennifer Vitak, an insurance professional with Liberty Mutual says, "You need to notify your insurance company if you are vacating your home, because your coverage may not remain the same once you're gone. If a customer knows their home is going to be vacant over 30 days, they should have it insured as a vacant home. For example, if there is a burst pipe due to the heat being turned off in the home, your claim could be in jeopardy, especially if it has been unoccupied for over 30 days. The premium will cost more due to the added risks; however, your home will be covered for losses."

In short, I want to emphasize the difficulties involved with buying and selling at the same time and advise you to avoid it if at all possible. If you can't avoid it, I guarantee you will NEVER do it again.

For your house to sell quickly, you want it to look its best. You don't want your home overloaded with unnecessary contents, so now is the time to begin weeding through your things and start making some hard decisions on what to keep and what to discard.

In the next chapter, I will review the best ways to evaluate and purge the excess contents in your home.

PART II:
CLEANING HOUSE

Chapter 4

Donate – Purge – Recycle

"One man's trash is another man's treasure."
~English Proverb

Now is a good time to start going through your things and purging some of your possessions. If you are moving into a bigger home, this is not as important, since you will be gaining storage space. However, take my advice and go through everything you have and make a point to donate, sell, or recycle what you don't want. It takes time and effort to sort through everything, but there is no sense paying movers to move stuff if it just doesn't have a place in your life anymore.

On our last big move, I thought I did a decent job of this, only to realize I had boxes and boxes of my old, unneeded possessions in the basement of the new home taking up valuable space. You will need to go through all of your items more than once to successfully purge many of your unwanted things. It's similar to sporting teams cutting players pre-season. They start with a few, and when they are done, they've cut dozens of players.

Once you start donating your goods, you will realize how great it feels knowing that others will get to enjoy the things for which you no longer have a use. It can be a very rewarding experience.

If you raised a family in your home, have lots of junk to prove it and are planning on downsizing, talk with your children to find out if they want any of the items they left behind, such as memorabilia, sporting equipment, baseball cards, dolls, furniture, etc. Give them an ultimatum to take their stuff or you are going to give it all to charity. This doesn't mean the charitable organizations will want everything, but it's a step in figuring out which items are staying with you or leaving for good.

Once you get a commitment from your family, you need to decide what you want to keep. This is not an easy process, as many of the things you own will have sentimental value and remind you of happy times with family members who are no longer with you. Remember, some of you are downsizing into a smaller place and need to lighten your load to be able to successfully move forward. You'll need to make a push to get rid of your many unnecessary possessions.

TIP: *Be sure to review the checklists in the appendix at the back of the book to help you with planning your move.*

Supplies
To help you get organized, I recommend purchasing plenty

of cardboard boxes, tall clothes boxes, markers, twine, packing tape and box cutters. You should also pick up some different colored round stickers from any general or office supply store. Use green to stick on items that you are definitely going to take with you. Use blue to put on items in which you are undecided. Use red for items you wish to sell. These are items where you think they will bring a tidy sum. Use white to stick on items you intend to donate to a local charity. Use brown for items you will have recycled or discarded. These are items which have no value and will not be accepted by charitable organizations, for example, an old color TV or old computer equipment. Of course, you can designate whichever color you'd like to the different categories. Just be sure to write down what each color represents so you won't forget.

Once you've labeled everything, it's time to start moving your stuff out. If you feel up to it, you can rent a truck to move many of your possessions out of the house, or you can pay someone else to deal with it. There are companies such as 1-800-Got Junk that will give you a same-day price and removal on anything you don't want. I have used them before on investment homes when I just couldn't seem to finish the job and wanted things removed quickly. I recommend removing the brown stickered (recycle/trash) items first. Then work on the white stickers (charity).

TIP: *I have successfully negotiated a lower fee with Got Junk after given their initial price. When they come out to give you an estimate, they are typically ready to pick up your stuff at that moment and would rather not waste their time and leave with no money or junk. Ask how much it will cost and* *see if you can't get the price down. It pays to haggle a little and you have nothing to lose.*

Once you've gotten rid of your unwanted possessions, trash, and recyclables, it is now time to focus on the nitty-gritty, such as your clothes. Where you will be moving will have a big impact on what clothes you will need to take with you. If you're headed to the Florida sun you probably won't be needing those flannel shirts or corduroy pants. However, if you're headed north, you will want to keep the cold weather clothes and boots.

Go through each article of clothing and put them into three piles.

<u>Pile #1</u> are the articles of clothing you absolutely must have, such as designer clothes.

<u>Pile #2</u> is your discard pile. These are articles of clothing you have not worn in years and probably will never want to wear again...until you get rid of them. ☺

<u>Pile#3</u> is the undecided pile. Try and make this pile as small as possible. If you really haven't worn these items in a while, it's probably best to put them into pile #2.

Charitable Organizations

Now that you have your piles separated, you can start to donate or sell pile #2. You can deal with this at the same time you allocate your home goods or you can treat them separately. I like to bring donated clothing to charities because it is much more manageable and fits easily in a car or SUV.

TIP: *Some charitable organizations such as The Cancer Federation and Salvation Army will pick up items at your house. This can save you precious time and energy. However, many will not pick up stained furniture. For a list of charitable organizations, their contact information and current status, go online to give.org. Remember to get a donation receipt that will provide evidence of your charitable donation to be used for tax purposes.*

Keep in mind there are companies and auction houses that will come to your house and give you an idea of what your furniture is worth. Some companies will purchase everything you don't want to keep and then they will sell or discard those same items, to alleviate you having to do the work. Of course, they're in the business of making a profit, so you will be paying for this service whether you know it or not. However, it can be a big stress reducer, knowing you don't have to hassle with it. To find organizations such as this in your area, Google *consignment shops* or *used furniture* for a list of outfits that might be willing to purchase all or much of your furniture and possessions.

Garage Sale

Lastly, you can always hold a garage sale to rid yourself of excess goods or pay someone else to hold one for you. This takes some effort in pricing the items and moving them into your garage or front lawn for shoppers to preview. I am not a big fan of garage sales. In fact, as of this writing, I have never had one. I prefer to donate excess goods rather than deal with the public and haggle over a $1 lamp at a garage sale. That's just my preference. Do what you are most comfortable with. The main goal is to get rid of excess items!

Storage Rentals

If for some reason, you find yourself in a quandary and are unwilling to part with many of your things, you can always buy some time and rent a storage unit to hold them until the pressure is off and you can go through your things at your leisure. Storage facilities are on the rise, so you should be able to find one nearby. Most will let you choose between climate-controlled rooms where your contents won't get too hot or too cold, or you may select the lesser expensive non-controlled units. Depending upon the quality of your goods, climate-controlled units may or may not be your best choice. Self-storage is a great way to rid yourself of lots of clutter in a short amount of time. I highly recommend this if you have a large number of things and need to lighten the load for showings. Keep in mind that once you go this route you will be paying a monthly fee to store items you may never use again.

It's important that you minimize your things so that your home doesn't look overrun with stuff. Selling, donating and recycling your unwanted possessions is a great way to *lighten the load*, while also being environmentally conscious.

In the next chapter, I will review the next steps on getting your house ready for showings. Grab a sponge and some Ajax and meet me on the next page.

Chapter 5

Down and Dirty

"If you think you are too small to make a difference, try sleeping with a mosquito."
~Dalai Lama

Now that you have a handle on your possessions, it is time to focus on getting your house ready for sale. Many homeowners will start working on areas of their home that won't make much of a difference in a sale, such as painting the garage. Not that this won't make the home look better, but the time spent could be better utilized tackling other projects which are much more important to a buyer.

The areas that should command most of your attention when getting your house ready to sell:

> ➢ Kitchen
> ➢ Interior Walls
> ➢ Bathrooms
> ➢ Master Bedroom
> ➢ Family room

> ➤ Exterior
> ➤ Roof

This is not to say the other areas of the home are not important and can be left in shambles. It just means you should start with the most scrutinized areas of the home first. This way, if you run out of time, you will have already completed the most significant rooms in your home.

Think of it as if you are going out on a big date. Are you going to be focusing your limited time on your toenails first, or are you going to start with your hair and outfit and then if you have time, start manicuring the little piggies?

If you think you will be listing your home with a real estate agent, now is a good time to have one or two visit your home and share their thoughts on the home's current condition and what they think could use some sprucing up. I have seen sellers devote far too much time on less important issues and neglect the major ones. For example, you don't want to be spending the bulk of your time with the basement and ignore the kitchen and baths. Best to have a seasoned professional assist you with your to-do list. It's important to prioritize because time probably isn't on your side as much as you think it is.

Kitchen

The kitchen is the most active room in the house. Let's face it, the kitchen is where delicious foods are prepared and is a great place to congregate with friends and family. The kitchen will get plenty of scrutiny because most buyers are looking for cleanliness, good storage capacity, lots of counter space, a spacious refrigerator, and a dishwasher and stove in good condition and within close proximity of each other. Kitchen designers call it a *work triangle*, where the refrigerator, sink, and stove are located in a triangular pattern. Buyers may also be looking for an eat-in kitchen, which is very popular, especially with families who have small children.

If your kitchen is smaller, don't fret. Just focus on enhancing the positives as much as you can. Thin out some of the contents in your cabinets to give it the feeling of spaciousness. This is not to say that you must completely empty out the cabinets. Just make it look as if you have room for the buyer's things, so they can imagine their kitchen equipment, spices, etc., fitting into your cupboards.

You should also clear some counter space to only include essential appliances, such as a toaster oven, coffeemaker, and microwave. Mixers, can openers, popcorn makers, crockpots, etc., should be temporarily stored to free up the precious countertop areas so buyers can envision lots of working space.

Keep in mind that clean sells! When car dealers acquire used cars into their inventory, what's one of the first things they do to it to help it sell? They detail the heck out of it! Interior dashboard, carpets, upholstery, clean windows, wax the exterior, clean the wheels, apply shine to the tires and add a pleasant interior scent. They are masters at making pre-owned cars sparkle and smell good. You need to be thinking the same thing when preparing your home for sale. I've never heard a buyer say, "I just don't care for this home, Dave, it's too clean." NEVER!

If buyers perceive your home as dirty, they may also think it has been poorly maintained. Their reasoning is as follows: If you can't take the time to properly clean your house when it is up for sale, then you probably didn't care to change the furnace filters on a regular basis, or clean the chimneys, gutters, or do much maintenance at all. Like it or not, this is what will run through the buyer's mind. I know this because I have toured homes with hundreds of buyers and have heard it firsthand.

While in the kitchen, take a look at the backsplash, especially around the stove. Is it splattered with grease? Time to do some scrubbing to get it clean. Also, look at the kitchen walls and ceiling. Are they in good shape or showing signs of heavy wear? You may need to repaint or at least touch up the paint where necessary. *Magic Erasers* are very handy at cleaning kitchen walls and doors. Just wet them and wipe the dirty surfaces. You will be amazed at what comes off of your walls. It really is like magic. Make sure you buy lots of them because they can go quickly if you have an abundance of smudged walls, doors and floorboards.

Take a good look at your kitchen appliances to ensure they're clean and in good shape. If they are older and run down, you may want to consider purchasing a package of appliances for a discount. November through January are wonderful months to get discounts on appliance packages. I have purchased stainless steel bundles to include a microwave, refrigerator, oven/stove and dishwasher for around $2,000. Buyers love new appliances and this is a great way to spruce up your kitchen. Once complete, you will have wished you had done it sooner.

You will also want to scrutinize your cabinets and drawers to make sure they are opening and closing properly.

Sometimes cabinet doors can get out of whack and need some adjusting done to the hinges. Also look at the finish of the cabinets. If they are dirty, you may want to clean them with a good cleaner. *Murphy's Oil Soap* is a wonderful wood cleaner that I have used in the past. It will clean your cabinets and leave them with a nice sheen. It is easy to use and doesn't have a harsh odor. If your cabinets are in really bad shape, you may want to consider having them refaced by replacing the doors or having all of the cabinets repainted. *Rust-Oleum* sells a very nice cabinet paint kit with many different colors to choose from. You can do this yourself or have a painter or handyman do it for you.

It is also very important that your kitchen has adequate lighting. Dark kitchens are not very appealing, especially if the buyers like to cook. Consider higher wattage LED bulbs if you feel your kitchen is too dark and be sure to replace any burned-out bulbs. If this doesn't help, you may want to consider adding a ceiling light to brighten up the area.

Lastly, how is the floor holding up? If it's finished hardwood it's probably showing signs of a wear pattern where much of the kitchen is frequently used. You should consider refinishing or at least polishing the wood floor. *Minwax* sells a floor refinisher I have successfully used in the past. It won't look as good as new, but it will look much better than before and it's easy to apply.

If your floor is tile, look for broken pieces and missing areas of grout. Although you may not think you have any, buyers will be coming in with a fresh set of eyes and will notice broken tiles right away. The more things they notice they feel they'll have to fix, the better chance that they will say, "Next," and move on to the following house for sale.

Let's face it, you are probably not looking to do a lot of work, on your next home right? Neither is the buyer of your current property. The more work that has already been completed, the more time they will have for themselves to move in and enjoy their new place. Home projects are a drag. They may look like fun in home-store commercials, but many of us know how difficult most projects are. They don't always go as planned, take much longer than anticipated and seldom turn out as good as we had hoped. Many buyers don't want to hassle with a bunch of home chores when first moving in. The more you can do ahead of time, the better chance you have of selling your home quickly and for more money. One adage I have used before is, *spend a dime to make a dollar.* Meaning, it costs money to do improvements, but the payoff in time and money can be well worth it due to a higher selling price.

Don't fall prey to pervasive thinking such as, "If they want the kitchen to look better, they can do it themselves, and then they can choose the colors and materials they want." I have heard this before and it is not prudent thinking. If you make repairs and improvements that are neutral in appearance and do not use wild colors or far-out schemes, you will not be spending your money in vain.

Interior Walls

Painting walls is the most inexpensive improvement you can do to your home. Your goal is to inspire the most possible number of buyers by having your home visually appealing, clean and neutral. For example, let's say 1 in 50 buyers like dark blue paint on the walls. Do you really want to have dark blue (or any dark-colored) paint in much of your home, waiting to appeal to the low percentage of buyers? Of course not.

While on the topic of paint, there are some other rules you should follow according to Steve Broujos, author of The Homeowners Guide to Surface Preparation for Interior House Painting. Steve says, "A quality paint job radiates a clean, fresh and cared-for look that attracts buyers, especially those who are looking for a house that's in move-in condition. When house painting for maximum profit, focus on color, sheen and surface preparation. Color is a handy tool to emphasize spaciousness. Light colors make rooms look larger, which is always a desirable selling point. White ceilings with an off-white color for walls and white trim is a way to accentuate the spaciousness of your house. It also provides a neutral background for colorful furnishings. If your house has small rooms, a light color palette is often a wise choice. Medium-shade colors for walls can be used when they complement flooring surfaces and any stone, brick, tile, counter-top or tile surfaces. Dark colors on walls make a room look smaller and should often be avoided, with the exception of accent walls."

Regarding paint sheen, Steve says, "Glossy paints reflect light which highlights surface defects, while flat paints reflect little, if any, noticeable light which minimizes surface defects. Most ceilings and walls should be painted with a gloss-free flat paint which will help your ceilings to look their best and allow you to touch up spots without having to repaint the entire ceiling. An eggshell or low-luster-finish paint, both of which have a slight sheen, is recommended for bathrooms as they need the added moisture protection that a paint's sheen provides. Trim surfaces, such as doors, door frames and baseboards, appear nicest if painted with white semi-gloss paint, giving it a timeless, classic look. It also allows surfaces to be more durable and easier to clean."

Steve says "Surface preparation is one of the most important parts of your painting job. Paint alone is not able to fix or conceal cracks, damaged surfaces or poorly sanded repairs. Savvy buyers recognize quality workmanship and are willing to pay top dollar for a property that has a well-crafted appearance."

Dated wallpaper should be minimized. Many buyers know how difficult wallpaper is to remove and will avoid homes where it is prevalent. Best to remove it yourself and have your home looking great ahead of time. I remember when we purchased our current home 17 years ago, it had every wall covered with paper. Before my family moved in, I painted it with my painter friend Steve after removing all of the wallpaper and dried glue. It was a blood, sweat and tears marathon and I was doing this in the evening after my real estate workday hours had ended. We spent many late nights peeling, scraping, sanding and painting that house. Funny how we can become nostalgic about things in the past that were a major pain in the butt at the time.

Weeks after finishing and moving into the home, we had family over and I remember walking into my freshly painted center hall entryway and seeing my kids and their nephew playing a game of run your shoes up the wall while standing on your hands to see how high you can go. %@#&*%!! OMG...did they not know how much money and time I had spent getting this place looking the way it did?? Did they not see the scuff marks they'd just put on my once-pristine wall?? The answer is NO, and they didn't really care. This is what kids do, and my wife reminded me of that before I sentenced them to their rooms for a lengthy imprisonment. I was fit to be tied, but I got over it and let "kids be kids" (within reason) and have fun in their new home. I could go on and talk about the $7,500 I spent on newly-refinished hardwood floors being roller-skated on by visiting children. I think you can imagine what was going through my head at the time. Once again, Mrs. H talked me out of "crucifying the little rascals" and into thinking, they're only floors that I paid %@#&*loads of money for.

Bathrooms

Bathrooms need to be sparkling clean, like when you check into a good hotel chain and your room's bath will have towels neatly hung, sink and toilet shiny and clean, floors immaculate, free of hair, and looking new. I know this is a tough task, especially when living in the home while trying to sell it, but it is an important one that will require some effort on your part. When buyers tour the master bathroom and see it sparkling and fresh to the point that they can envision themselves bathing there, you are much closer to making a sale. If, on the other hand, they get a feeling of "Eww, look at all the hair on the floor and scum in the shower," they will be turned off and it will have a negative effect on the rest of their tour. I've heard this first-hand from buyers. Sentences such as, "How can they live like this?" and "If this is how it looks now, imagine how it looked before they put it on the market."

Bathroom cleanliness is paramount, especially because of the potential presence of bacteria and viruses. Imagine walking into your doctor's office restroom and seeing hair everywhere, mold in the toilets, and sink and smudges on the mirror and walls. You would probably be changing doctors. Buyers will feel the same way about your house. Clean is paramount, don't neglect this important fact.

If your bathroom was built before 1980, there is good chance it could stand some minor updating. If you have the old ceramic wall tile that came in a plethora of colors including pink, black, grey, yellow, red, white and light green, you should consider having your tiles re-glazed. You can do it yourself or hire a professional to do it for you. It is basically brushing or spraying on the new glaze after doing a bunch of prep work. However, if you do it wrong, it could expose imperfections, such as little surface bumps that don't look appealing. Just Google *professional tile glazing* along with your city/state and you will find companies that specialize in this. It is much cheaper than replacing the wall tile, which is very labor-intensive.

Some of the older floor tiles are currently in retro and should be just fine. Small black and white tiles have become very popular again. If your floor tile is really dated, you may want to consider replacing it. Re-tiling over top of it will be your less expensive option. I did this in our current home, and it turned out very nice. I just needed to replace the marble threshold with a higher one to accommodate for the increased height of the floor.

If you really want to save some money, you can purchase the 12" x 12" self-adhesive vinyl floor tiles. Just use regular scissors to cut them to fit, peel the adhesive and stick in place. You will also want to wash the floor and wipe it with some rubbing alcohol to help the vinyl tiles adhere. I accomplished this in our previous home and it turned out very well. These tiles also look nice in a laundry room since it gives it a smooth and clean surface.

While in the bathroom, take a good look at your sink, vanity, mirror, toilet, and shower/tub area along with the grout. If they are showing signs of age or have stains, you might want to consider replacing some of them. This is especially important in the master bathroom where your potential buyers will be checking it out very carefully. Just as new appliances can really spruce up a kitchen, a new sink and faucet and fresh caulk can go a long way in the bathroom. If you are only replacing the sink and not the shower/tub hardware, you should keep with the same type of materials. Since most toilets are porcelain, they can be cleaned up pretty well, unless they have been exposed to well water, which can do a number on them. It's probably best to replace them if you can't get them sparkling clean.

Also, take a look at the current bathroom lighting. Are the fixtures dated, such as large globe-type bulbs? If so, you should consider replacing your lights. *Lowes* has a tremendous selection in most of their stores and at very reasonable prices. Lights are a relatively inexpensive enhancement that shouldn't be overlooked. Another bathroom improvement is to add a new shower rod that bows out away from the tub. This gives the illusion of a larger shower and the curtain will not be brushing up against you as you bathe. Many hotels have switched to these for that very reason. New shower curtains are an inexpensive upgrade that can really enhance a bathroom. Also, consider displaying some of your nicest bath towels folded neatly along with washcloths and hand towels.

Master Bedroom

The master bedroom should be clean, with minimal clutter. You want to have plenty of extra room in your closets to give the illusion of space. Clothes should be neatly folded, and hanging clothes arranged in smart order, such as shirts, then pants, then short dresses, long dresses, etc. Make sure you don't have lots of unwanted shoe boxes and old shoes in the closets. It's a great time to donate those shoes you never wear anymore. Remaining shoes should be carefully positioned and not strewn about the floor. I like putting shoes onto stepped platforms (shoe condos) where they are all in one place.

The bed needs to be made every day that there are showings. Bedroom knickknacks should be kept to a minimum and all of the furniture should be dusted regularly. Buyers can sense when a seller has their act together and runs their household in an orderly fashion. I have heard buyers say things like, "Wow, this person is really super organized. They take very good care of their things."

Remember to dust the picture frames, artificial plants, and assorted knickknacks. You want to start minimizing your personal photos so they are not overwhelming. It's perfectly fine to have a few family photos around the house, but don't overdo it. Remember, you are staging the home for potential buyers, not you. Lots of pictures in a house may just add to the visual clutter. When you get to your next destination, you can put all of your pictures back and start enjoying them again. This is only temporary.

Family Room

It's time to unload many of those VCR movies you purchased along with your cassette tapes. Goodwill is a fine destination for these items. Consider organizing any remaining DVD's, and CD's so they are not a distraction. Put away any toys, games and other playthings that can be a trip hazard. It's all right to have a few toys out, but don't overdo it.

You should vacuum and thoroughly clean the family room throughout, dust the TV and vacuum behind it with the suction hose to get all the dust bunnies and cobwebs which may have accumulated back there. I know from experience that it can get pretty nasty behind the TV. If your TV is mounted, all the better. Flat-screen televisions can make great inclusions, especially if they look good and you don't want the hassle of removing them. Buyers like freebies such as nice electronics, refrigerators, washer, and dryers. The less they have to do, the better chance they will want your house as their own.

If you have hardwood floors with dark stains, these are typically areas where pets have urinated. These stains sink deep into the hardwood, making them practically impossible to sand out. I have experienced this with investment properties and learned the best way to rectify this is to have a professional flooring contractor cut out the stained areas and replace it with the same type of wood, which will need to be sanded, color stained, and coated with polyurethane.

I have also seen floors stained a dark color to try and hide the pet marks. Doing so can make your floors display dust and dirt much more frequently and thus make it difficult to keep showroom clean for selling. Your other options would be an area rug or wall-to-wall carpeting.

TIP: *It's a good idea to remove any materials you have lying around your home that others may find offensive. These can include risqué items such as movies, or things of a political nature, like posters or propaganda. Although your house feels natural to you, its possessions could push people away who do not share your politics, religion, or other interests.*

Exterior

"After seeing the outside, I just don't have any desire to go inside, so let's just go to the next house." I have heard buyers say this many times when I'm touring with them. We pull up to a house and find it overgrown with weeds and unkept bushes taking over the place, broken shutters, a storm door that won't close and a gutter hanging loose. If a buyer sees the outside in disarray, they will assume the inside is even worse and they won't want to waste any more of their time. Agents will be happy to forgo an unkempt home, knowing the chances are slim on selling it. I've even had buyers comment on the trees saying things such as, "That one looks as if it could fall on the house at any time." Or, "It's going to cost a small fortune to remove all of those old bushes and trees."

A good way for a seller to tackle this is to go outside with a clipboard and write down anything you think may be unappealing to a buyer. You might even want to take some pictures since we often overlook things when viewing them live, only to notice abnormalities later when looking at the photos.

Also, take a good look at your lawn. Is it neatly cut and edged at the sidewalk and driveway? Do the bushes need trimming away from the house? On one of the investment properties I acquired, I purchased some green dye to help spruce up the lawn. The property had been vacant for a long time and it was a quick way to make it look more attractive. I also added seed, so the lawn would improve with a little time.

Fresh mulch can go a long way toward your flower beds' appearances. Adding some fresh annuals out front is a wonderful way to welcome your visitors. Hanging plants on the front porch is also a nice touch. Be sure to clean any cobwebs you see. An easy way to do so is with a broom, and then use a paper towel to remove the webs from the bristles when done. If you have a lot of them, you might want to use a shop-vac to suck them all up.

Be sure to check the driveway and walkways for uneven cracks. Certain types of buyer financing will require raised cracks to be repaired before the house can settle, so best to check it out now. See Chapter 20 for additional information regarding the different types of financing and how it can affect your home sale.

While you're outside, take a look at the gutters. Are they overflowing with leaves, are plants growing there, or are the gutters and downspouts in good shape? If not, you know what to do.

Roof

Are the shingles showing signs of curling and losing much of their surface? This is a sign of age and that the roof is nearing the end of its useful life. You have several options if you want to be proactive.

Option #1: Disclose the age of the roof in the seller's disclosure and note that you have had no issues and that it is functioning as intended. Only state the aforementioned if this is accurate.

Option #2: Re-shingle over the existing layer of shingles, provided there is currently only one layer and that your local government allows more than one layer. This will save you in labor costs because the roofers won't need to tear off the old roof.

Option #3: Do a complete tear-off of the old shingles and replace with new, while also replacing any warped underlayment (plywood). This option is the most expensive, but looks the best and is most favored by buyers.

Option #4: Offer an upfront credit at closing towards a new roof. The buyer's lender/mortgage company will probably not want to see this in writing and may want it worded such as, *Seller to provide Buyer with $XXXX in settlement assistance at time of closing.* This is much more underwriter friendly and shouldn't pose a problem.

There is a chance your roof is fine and it just has algae growing all over it. This is not attractive to look at and it is not good for the life of the shingles. You can Google *roof cleaning* in your area to see a list of area contractors that specialize in this. I had this done on a property of mine because the roof was visible from the second level of the home and it looked terrible. I paid to have it cleaned and it was well worth it. Most of the shingles looked like new when they were finished. There were some areas that had to be retreated due to heavy moss growth, but the company came back and redid those areas for free under warranty. Afterwards, it was ready for showings!

The backyard should be tidy with toys and equipment kept to a minimum. Buyers are looking for backyards that provide them with room for entertainment and some privacy. Make sure you remove any pet piles so they don't negatively impact the buyers' opinion. Get rid of any old tires, broken toys, and furniture, along with anything else that is an eyesore.

Take a look at your front windows and shutters. Is there any peeling paint, cobwebs, or gaps around the windows where the caulk has worn away? If so, you will want to rectify this before selling. It's also a good idea to put out some attractive doormats (front and back) which will not only look nice but allow buyers to wipe their feet when entering. You should also put mats inside the home for the same purpose. If there are no inside mats, you will find wet footprints and shoe marks throughout the house after showings. Taking all of these steps is a chore, but well worth the effort if you want to sell your home for maximum value.

If your property needs lots of repairs, you can always sell it in *as-is* condition. Kevin Hollerman, sales manager with Movement Mortgage, says, "Fixer-upper homes are a great way to promote renovation financing programs available to buyers, such as FHA 203K. This alleviates the need for repairs to be done by the seller in order to prepare to list the property, since the buyer will be purchasing the home with the current defects."

You will also want to take a look at your furnace to make sure it has a clean filter. Dirty filters can entice home inspectors to recommend a cleaning. If you're really feeling ambitious, pop the furnace cover and see how it looks inside. I will occasionally vacuum out any debris or cobwebs that have accumulated. Inspectors will also be looking at this.

It goes without saying your home should be clean and free of noticeable defects. Windows should be sparkling and crystal clear. Lights should all be working and all burnt out bulbs should be replaced. Doors should all be functional and walls free of scuff marks. Performing the majority of tasks listed in this chapter will ensure a more timely and profitable sale.

In the next chapter, I will review nine potential deal killers that may already exist in your home. It's best to know now if you have any of them so you can determine the best course of action.

Chapter 6

Nine Deadly Deal Killers

"I can accept failure...but I can't accept not trying."
~Michael Jordon

It seems like every year that I have been involved in real estate, the rules and regulations just keep getting tougher. One year, for example, posed a problem with bad imported drywall. Because of a hurricane that hit Florida especially hard, the U.S. supply of drywall was dwindling so the U.S. imported drywall from China. Unfortunately, the drywall contained excess levels of sulfur, which over time is known to corrode electrical wires and thus create problems.

Although this was mainly found in the Southern United States, it is just another example of change and how it can affect home sales. Owners that had repaired their homes with this defective drywall ended up having to replace all of it along with much of their wiring. Now many seller's disclosures ask if you have any knowledge of such drywall in your home.

There are other deficiencies you should know about and verify to see if your property has been negatively affected by any of them so you can be proactive and avoid imminent headaches later.

The topics to which I am referring alphabetically are:

1. Aluminum Wiring
2. Asbestos
3. Buried Oil Tanks
4. Lead
5. Polybutylene Plumbing
6. Radon
7. Septic Tanks
8. Stucco
9. Wells

Aluminum Wiring

A.W. came about during the seventies when the price of copper became very expensive due to the Vietnam War. A copper replacement was needed and A.W. fit the bill since it is an excellent, inexpensive conductor of electricity. The issue with A.W. is that it expands and contracts more than copper and this consequently can cause connections to loosen up over time. If fittings get too lose, a gap can form, which can cause electrical arcing, and hence lead to a potential fire.

Thankfully, there are now aluminum rated electrical switches and outlets which are specifically designed for A.W. Other repair options include having an electrician *pigtail* the aluminum ends with copper wiring via a connector and then have the copper wire affixed to an outlet or switch. This is termed the *Copalum crimp method* and it requires an electrician who is certified to do it. It is a more expensive route than replacing all the outlets and switches since it requires a special tool and fittings for attaching the copper wire to the aluminum wire. The final and most expensive route is to replace all of the existing A.W. with copper wires. This is a very labor-intensive job, having to switch to all new wires throughout the home.

An easy way to tell if you have A.W. is to have an electrician take an outlet cover off and pull it out of the box to see what color the attached wires are. If they are copper-colored, you're good. If they are silver in color, they are most likely aluminum. To be sure, they should check more than one area of your home. If you do have A.W., at the very minimum, you'll need to disclose it, and you should take added precautions and seriously consider professionally replacing all of the switches and outlets with *UL certified* ones rated for aluminum wiring. Costs to replace outlets and switches can cost approximately $300-$1,000, depending upon how many you have. Pig-tailing can run up to $10 to $15 per wire.

Asbestos

This was once a booming product since asbestos was used in many areas of home building, to include pipe insulation, flooring tiles, ceiling tiles and exterior siding. I have been told by countless home inspectors that exterior siding is perfectly safe if left alone.

Even so, you need to be aware of potential roadblocks in the sale of your home so you can maximize its value. If you have old flooring tile, it is probably best to have it professionally removed. These tiles were often glued to solid slab foundations (concrete) and they will need to be scraped up with a specialized tool. These tiles are very heavy in weight and should be disposed of properly, according to local government protocol.

Pipe insulation with asbestos was common in older homes, so take a look in the basement to see if any of your plumbing pipes or air ducts were wrapped in asbestos. In most instances, it will appear a chalky white color. Do not touch it, or it could release fibers into the air. If you think you have asbestos insulation, contact a licensed professional who works in asbestos removal. They will come out and test the materials and provide you with options, such as encapsulating the insulation, so it does not shed any airborne fibers. They will also give you the option of removing it completely.

Just because you are not aware of asbestos, does not mean buyers and their agents will be oblivious to it. It is well known in the real estate community and most home inspectors will be on the lookout for it. It's best to know in advance what you're dealing with and get a head start on remediating it. Costs will vary depending upon how much asbestos you have and what will be required to bring remove or encapsulate it.

Buried Oil Tanks

Sometimes sellers will be unaware of buried oil tanks on properties they own since there was no disclosure when they purchased the home. The main problem with buried oil tanks is that they are prone to leak oil. The 275-gallon tanks only have an approximate 50-year life expectancy and if the house is 75 years old, there are bound to be issues. Oil is a hazardous material that, when spilled is a danger to the environment. In my state, any known leaking tanks need to be professionally removed with government oversight to make sure that the ground is clean of contaminants.

If you think you may have a buried oil tank, now is the time to have it permanently put to rest. A good home inspector can sometimes discover the presence of a buried oil tank, so it's best to be proactive. Some areas of the country will allow the tank to be filled with sand to prevent contamination. Other areas will require the tank to be completely removed. In any event, once a buyer and his or her real estate agent find out about a buried oil tank that has not been properly dealt with, they will be off to the next home, due to future unknown costs to remedy the situation.

If you do have a buried tank and would like more information, contact the state and county where you live for advice. Once the tank is properly abandoned or removed, you will want to provide written documentation to the buyers to demonstrate that it was handled properly as required by local code. Costs to remove tanks could easily exceed $2,500 since heavy equipment is usually required.

Lead

Lead contamination in real estate can sometimes be found in the paint of older homes built prior to 1978. It can be especially prevalent in old city homes where peeling paint falls onto the ground and is consumed by children. Apparently, the paint chips have a sweet taste that children have been known to consume if they are hungry or curious. It's one of the reasons why certain types of financing will not allow peeling paint in any of their homes even if the house was built after 1978, when lead paint was abolished in residential construction.

Some areas of the home where peeling paint is most common is on bathroom ceilings, where constant moisture will cause it to peel. Peeling paint is also prevalent on older wooden windows that take a beating from the sun. As a property owner wanting to sell a home, you do not want to have any peeling paint in your house regardless of its age. One exception to the rule is if you are selling the property in *as-is condition,* such as an estate sale where you sell the house for a lower price and forgo any repairs.

If you would like to find out if your home contains lead, you can purchase a lead testing kit at local home stores and test a few areas of the home to see if any lead is present. If it is not present, you can treat it as you normally would. If lead is present, you should speak with a licensed lead abatement contractor to discuss your options. More information can be found on The Environmental Protection Agencies (EPA) website at *www.epa.gov.*

The second form of lead exposure that has been drawing a lot of attention lately is from drinking water. It has become an even hotter topic lately with fiascos occurring in several U.S. cities with public water testing at high lead levels. Apparently, much of this was due to old municipal pipes which contained lead, which then leached into the main water supply.

If you want to be proactive, you can purchase a water test kit at a local home store and test your water. Simply take a water sample with the kit provided and mail it into the lab. Within a week or so, you will receive the results. If they come back with elevated levels of lead, you will then want to test the same water source taken from a different place, such as a newer public building, and have it also tested. If the other source is negative, you know your house is the cause and is more than likely due to something such as lead solder that was used to connect the supply pipes. Discuss any pipe replacements with your local plumber.

Polybutylene Plumbing

Polybutylene (Poly-B) is a flexible plastic resin piping that was used between 1978-1995 as a substitute for copper, which is expensive and more labor-intensive to install. Unlike rigid copper pipes, Poly-B is flexible and can be easily fished through walls. The issue with Poly-B piping is that it is prone to leak. Most Poly-B piping is gray in color and should say Polybutylene right on the pipe. However, I have seen Poly-B piping without it written on the pipe. If you think you have it, get an estimate for its replacement with a new and improved flex pipe such as PVC or Pex. Or, you can simply disclose that it is currently being used in your home on the seller's disclosure document and let the buyers know they are purchasing it as-is. The replacement pipe can typically be fished through the walls alongside the older Poly B piping, which will be removed once the new pipes are attached to the water supply. Expect to spend a minimum of $2,500 on replacement, depending upon the areas affected.

Radon

Radon is a naturally-occurring gas that is produced by the biological breakdown of radium below the earth's surface. It is an odorless, colorless, tasteless, radioactive gas that is a health hazard and has been linked to lung cancer. The Environmental Protection Agency (EPA) has set the acceptable limits of radon to be 4.0 pCi/L and below. Anything that tests below this level is acceptable and anything testing above this level is considered unsafe. Radon testing can be done with kits purchased at home improvement stores or is done professionally by many home inspectors. Basements are more likely to have higher levels of radon because they are below ground and closer to the source. Homes without basements will be less likely to have elevated radon levels.

It has become common practice to remediate radon fairly inexpensively in basements where the levels have tested high. Many new home builders are preemptively installing radon mediation systems in their homes to prevent high readings and broken sales contracts. They are relatively simple in design, but require expertise to install properly. I have seen systems cost between $750 and $1,200.

Septic Tanks

Rarely have I ever seen a septic tank pass an inspection without needing any repairs or alterations. Dealing with these tanks is a dirty business that many contractors dare not venture into, which keeps the competition down and prices up. If you are selling a home with a septic tank, I highly recommend you have a pre-emptive inspection to take a look into your system and make sure it is functioning properly. You will want to have the tanks pumped beforehand so they can really see inside the tank. Chances are it will need to have something done, so now is the time to fix it.

Buyers may want to have a hydraulic load test done on the system to help determine if the drain field is working properly. This test involves pumping approximately 500 gallons of water into the septic system to gauge how efficiently the system distributes it. You may want to consider having this test done ahead of time, as well, although it is somewhat expensive and not all buyers will have this test done. Keep in mind that septic testing is very weather permitting and it's important that it be conducted when it is not raining.

Once everything has been inspected and repaired, you can provide the proper documentation and disclose to the buyers that the *septic tank was just professionally inspected and repaired.* Most buyers will be thrilled they won't have to pay for an additional inspection and you can rest easy knowing that this is one less thing you have to worry about.

I have seen septic repairs cost as much as $25,000, so you can see why I've included it in this chapter. Be proactive and see what's percolating down below so you can get a head start on selling your home for maximum profit.

Stucco

Synthetic stucco or EIFS (exterior insulation and finish system) has gotten lots of attention lately. Apparently, moisture can get behind the stucco in certain areas of the home and create mold, mildew and wood rot. If you have a stucco home that was built around 1990 and later, there is a fair chance that your home will have issues, whether you know it or not.

Stucco has been a hot button issue in the real estate industry and is only getting hotter with repair estimates that can exceed $100,000. In my area of business, it is now commonplace to have a stucco inspection before listing a house for sale. If for some reason you don't wish to do so, buyers may take a pass on it or offer to purchase your home contingent upon a satisfactory stucco inspection completed at the seller's expense-which means you may as well have it completed now, since you will probably have to pay for it anyway.

Stucco inspections can run over $1,000 and are very comprehensive since it entails drilling into the stucco at different areas of the house and taking core samples along with moisture readings to determine if the stucco has been compromised. Jeff Hunt, a certified stucco inspector and franchise owner of Pillar to Post Home Inspectors, says, "It is important to check the lower corners of windows for any

gaps and to press on the sealant to see if it is firm. If any of your windows have staining under them, referred to as stucco tears, you may have algae growing in the stucco." A logical solution would be power washing, right?
WRONG! He says, "The worst thing you can do to stucco stains is spraying high-pressure water on the stains." He recommends contacting a licensed stucco inspector to have your home professionally inspected before things can get out of hand.

Currently, most educated buyers won't touch a stucco home without it being professionally tested. If you are going to be selling your property soon and it has a stucco exterior, you will want to get your home tested.

If your home tests fine, then you can let all potential buyers know that you were proactive, and provide them with the stucco report showing that your house tested clean. If the report shows issues, you will want to hire a licensed contractor who specializes in stucco repairs and have those issues addressed as soon as possible. Most likely, the repairs will be centered around your windows and doors. It's also fairly common for some stucco homes to not contain proper kick-out flashing on the roof to divert water away from the exterior walls.

Once you have your inspection report and/or repair receipts, you can provide them to interested buyers to eliminate their concerns about your home's stucco. The sooner the issue is addressed, the cheaper it will cost. Like the old commercial says, "You can pay me now, or you can pay me (more money) later." There have been lawsuits against EIFS, so check and see if you can join an existing suit if you find that your home has issues.

Wells

Owners of private wells are responsible for ensuring that their water is safe from contaminants. Private wells should be checked every year for mechanical problems, cleanliness, and the presence of coliform bacteria, nitrates and any other contaminants of local concern. A local health department or water well systems professional can help ensure delivery of high-quality water from an existing well or, if needed, help locate and construct a new well in a safer area.

It is not uncommon to have well water tests come back with various contaminants in the water. Seldom have I seen a well that didn't need to be "shocked" with chlorine to cleanse the water back to an acceptable reading. However, I have not yet experienced the same high repair costs that I have seen with many septic systems. Well problems typically amount to quality of water issues, along with the condition of the well pump to ensure it is adequately pumping enough supply to the home and at the correct water pressure. Pumps last approximately 8-10 years and can cost upwards of $2,000 to replace. Other criteria inspectors will be looking at is the well depth along with its current water supply. Rarely have I seen inadequate water amounts, which can be a good indicator that another well may have to be drilled.

Another item I occasionally see fail is the well cap. A good cap will not allow bugs or anything else to enter inside the opening, so it's important to have the right one. It's a good idea to be proactive by having both the well and septic inspected prior to listing your property for sale. This way you can market both the septic and well's benefits by stating in the disclosures that *both have passed a recent inspection, receipts provided at the buyer's request.* This assures buyers who would otherwise decide against spending the money on their own well inspection, which is music to your ears.

Although solar panels are not on this list, due to their technical nature, they deserve to be mentioned here. Andrew P. Taylor, an attorney with Copeland Taylor, LLC foresees future issues with the sale of homes with solar panels since the panels are typically leased from the solar company. He says, "Because of the complexities regarding the transfer of the solar panels and the need for third party approval by the solar company, this process should be undertaken early in the home sale process in order to avoid settlement delays." If you do have a solar system, best to contact them now concerning the transference of the equipment to a new owner.

Knowing if you have any of the previous issues with your home can help you determine how best to handle any of them before your house goes on the market and under contract with a buyer. Once this occurs, there will be lots of scrutiny from buyers, their agents and home inspectors monitoring you every step of the way. Best to take care of it ahead of time to avoid the *too many cooks in the kitchen,* syndrome, where it is more difficult to get things done.

In the next chapter, I will cover if you should call in professional help to review your property and suggest repairs and improvements. Two heads really can be better than one.

PART III:
PROFESSIONAL
GUIDANCE

Chapter 7

Call in the Cavalry

"Without cavalry, battles are without result."
~Napoleon Bonaparte

You may want to get some professional advice
sooner, rather than later to gather ideas on what you should
be improving and what doesn't really matter. When you live
in a home for a long time, everything starts to blend together
and you may lose perspective concerning its condition,
relative to how other people, such as buyers will see it.
Oftentimes if you ask friends and family for their opinions,
they will be too nice to give you any objective feedback, so
it's best to have an impartial third party review it with you.
Many homeowners don't even realize that their house has a
distinct odor until they come home after a long vacation.

When you vacate, you will inadvertently leave some
things behind because you hardly notice them anymore. For
example, on our last move, we left a hanging picture along
with some other items because they seemed to blend in with
the house. The buyer's agent ended up calling us and asking

if we wanted these items back...heck, yeah! A fresh set of eyes coming through your house will observe things you never thought of or hadn't noticed in a long time.

Water Stains

I remember doing a pre-listing tour through a home and seeing a couple of dark spots on the ceiling that were undoubtedly caused by a water leak of some kind. I stopped and stared at the water stains, not saying anything. Eventually the seller asked, "Should we do anything with that? We had a leaky bathtub years ago and got it replaced. Do you think we should fix the ceiling?" "Why yes, yes I do think you should fix the ceiling and disclose it, because if you don't, the buyers will think the problem has not been repaired and that they will be the ones who have to deal with it."

Another example was when I was walking around the outside of a home, and I looked up and noticed some missing pieces of vinyl siding. The homeowner never even noticed they were gone. I just stared at the missing pieces of siding, waiting for the homeowner to explain what I was seeing. Eventually he said, "Not sure when that happened. I guess we should fix that." "Yes, you should fix it if you want to get the maximum amount of money for your home."

Let's face it, a seller does not have to fix a darned thing if they don't want to. They can keep the water stains or leave the missing siding as-is. They can even have trees lying horizontally across the backyard. And yes, your house will still sell. It will just take longer and won't sell for its maximum value because there are too many things wrong with it.

The more items a buyer feels needs to repaired the lower the offer price will be. If your house is so far gone in needed repairs, it may not even be eligible for proper financing such as FHA or even conventional financing. This means if a buyer is going to finance it at all, it will have to be a special type of home improvement financing such as FHA 203K, where the home is deemed unfinanceable by typically means and it is going to have to undergo repairs via a coordinated schedule, overseen by the mortgage lender where the buyer obtains contractor estimates on repairs that will be approved or denied by the lender.

In short, if you want to maximize your profits and minimize your pains in selling the home, do some needed repairs now. Your local real estate agent will be happy to review your house with you at no cost and give you their opinions as to what should be done and what would be considered overkill or a waste of your time and money.

I have saved homeowners lots of money by informing them that their current improvement plan won't make much of any difference at all and will hardly be noticed.

Pre-Market Home Inspection

Some agents insist their sellers have a pre-market home inspection to determine what issues their house currently has. Other agents feel this is unnecessary and can potentially cause more harm than good, since most states require all defects to be disclosed. I think this should be handled on a case-by-case basis, since properties and seller circumstances are all different.

I lean more toward limiting pre-inspections to more expensive homes where the owner has lived in the property for over 10 years and may have defects of which they are unaware. Less expensive homes don't seem to justify the cost of the inspections.

I have seen buyers spend lots of money on home inspections and be very disappointed with the results, but feel committed to purchase the property because of the money they've invested. If a seller has a pre-listing inspection and merely discloses all of the defects without fixing them, it may turn off a buyer from the start before they feel any attachment to the home.

Ask a real estate professional their thoughts when they first come out to look at your house. Much of it depends upon the age, condition of the property and how long the owner has lived in it.

Over-Improvements

Months ago, I was asked to give a seller a market analysis on his home. He walked me through the property and then showed me the basement, which he was still in the process of finishing. He was adding a full bath, a movie theatre and a game room. It looked as if it had cost him a small fortune. I asked him approximately how much money he had spent, and he informed me it was around $25,000. I then asked, "Why are you spending all of this money on finishing your basement if you are moving?" He said he wanted to finish the basement to add livable square footage and increase the home's value.

Gulp! I politely informed him that a finished basement's square footage is not given the same value as above grade, livable square footage. That got his attention. "Say what?" he replied.

I repeated myself, saying, "Appraisers don't give the same value for finished basement square footage as they do for above ground square footage, such as your kitchen, family room, office, living room, dining room and bedrooms."

He then asked, "So why am I spending all this money to finish my basement?!" He was now very frustrated and angry.

"I wish you had called me before you started this project," I said, "Because I would have recommended you not do so." I then informed him that buyers would love the basement and would likely be willing to pay extra for it. There is no doubt it will help you sell the home faster. However, you may not get your $25,000 back in the selling process after its appraised.

Steam was now coming out of his ears, and I felt like the King's messenger who'd just given the King some really bad news. Not a good feeling.

We discussed his basement for a while and I asked if he thought the basement money would have been better invested in an IRA, mutual fund or some other type of investment. He said it probably would do better in the stock market. Of course, timing is everything and he realized his error in judgment. Having learned a valuable lesson, he decided to rent his home in hopes of future neighborhood appreciation.

Appraisers will not give a lot of added value to under grade, basement-type dwellings. It does not amount to the same dollar for dollar comparison that finished rooms above ground typically go for, which in my area is around $150 to $200 per sq. ft. For example, a home with 1,000 sq. ft of above ground finished area with no garage will be worth approx. $150,000 to $225,000 provided it is in a decent location. If you finished 300 sq. ft of the basement, you would be lucky to get an added appraised value of $10,000, which is only $33 per sq. ft. Oftentimes sellers think that because they invested $20,000 into their basement, that they will get it all back when the home is sold. Even if the buyer is willing to pay the higher amount, the appraiser will most likely value the home for less than what it sold for, which means the bank will only finance a percentage of the appraised value and not its selling price, and thus the sale could be in jeopardy.

For example, let's say 123 Main Street sells for $200,000 and the buyer is taking out a 95% loan, or $190,000. If the appraised value comes in at $193,000, $7,000 shy of its selling price, the bank will only lend the buyer 95% of $193,000 (appraised value) which equals $183,350. This means the buyer is going to have to come up with much more of their own money to purchase the home for $200,000. In this case, they will need to bring a total of $16,650 ($200,000 - $183,350). Before the low appraisal they only needed to bring $10,000 ($200,000 - $190,000). Lastly, these figures do not include closing fees such as transfer tax, attorneys' fees, etc. which will increase the buyer's costs.

In this example, what do you think the buyer is going to do? I can tell you from experience they are going to tell the seller they will only pay what the house is worth, the $193,000 that it was appraised for. If the seller says no, the two parties can negotiate an agreement, or the buyer can have their lender write a letter stating they do not have the additional funds needed to close and therefore cannot obtain a loan to purchase the house. Since the purchase offer is most likely contingent upon the buyers getting a loan, as the terms state in most contracts, the buyer's agent then presents this letter to the listing agent along with a signed release asking for their deposit money back.

What does this all mean? It means, *don't spend large sums of money on home improvements that are not going to provide added value.* Remember, the two biggest areas of return on your investment are the kitchens and baths, and even in those areas you can over-improve if you are not careful.

For example, say I own a property that is worth $200,000 which is surrounded by other properties that are worth approximately the same amount. I spend $95,000 on a remodeled kitchen. Am I going to be able to sell that property for $295,000? I may be able to find a buyer for the property, but if they are taking out a loan that requires an appraisal, when the appraiser comes out, he or she will most likely realize the house is *over-improved*, meaning the neighborhood does not support the added improvements of the home and it will most likely be appraised lower than $295,000.

In other words, it may only appraise for around $245,000, which means I'm not going to get back what I paid for the improvements because the area where the home is located does not support those higher values. Some owners are okay with that fact because they plan on dying in the house. Others are unaware, because there is simply no one to warn them. Don't fall into this trap. If you find yourself wanting to convert your home into the Taj Mahal or want to add another 1,000 sq. ft of living space, it may be best to move into an area of similar type and sized properties that supports the value then to risk over-improving your existing property. This is where an experienced real estate agent can help you assess if it's worth your while to do certain improvements.

Getting some early advice on your property can get you headed in the right direction. Make sure you put your time and effort into the areas of you home that will actually make a difference, and don't over-improve areas of less importance.

In the next chapter, I will discuss the pros and cons of selling the property yourself. Will you actually save money? Or could it cost you money in not knowing some of the pitfalls? Grab your calculator and meet me on the next page!

Chapter 8

To FSBO or Not to FSBO

"Timid salesmen have skinny kids."
~Zig Ziglar

In this chapter, I will review the pros and cons of *for sale by owner*, (FSBO) and help you decide which scenario is best for you.

Even though I have been licensed in real estate since 1998, I have always listed my investment and personal properties with a broker. Of course, I use my current broker, along with myself as the listing agent. My point is that I don't sell it FSBO. You may be thinking, "Why would anyone with over two decades of real estate selling experience list their own home for sale with a broker?" The answer is simple-because the Multiple Listing Service (MLS) is the quickest way to expose your home to the greatest number of qualified buyers.

Of course, I would entertain offers on the investment properties while they were being remodeled; however, I always ended up listing them. Time is money, and the longer it takes to sell your home, the more expensive it can become, due to the holding costs of sitting on a vacant home to include the loan, insurance, utilities, property taxes, lawn maintenance, snow removal, liability, stress and more.

Buyer Preferences

Most buyers prefer to work with a third party, such as a buyer's agent rather than work directly with the seller. They don't want to be in the position of having to ask for repairs to be done or negotiating a lower price directly with the owner. They would much prefer to go through an agent and have them do the dirty work for them.

TIP: *Be sure to check out the **For-Sale Checklist** and **Closing Checklist** located in the Appendix section at the back of the book. These will provide you with a step-by-step guide on how to show and sell your property.*

Many for sale by owners (FSBO) lack sales experience and are not suitable for showing buyers around the house. For example, I took a couple into a FSBO home because my buyers really wanted to see it. Once we got inside, the seller insisted that he lead the tour. While looking at the home, he practically pointed out every screw, doorknob, and lightbulb he replaced. We were on our seventh house of the tour, that afternoon and it was exhausting being slowly led around while having to hear the seller drone on about the inconsequential improvements he had made to the property. Since I was present, I was able to corner my buyers and quietly ask them if they had any interest in this home. They shook their heads and I graciously told the seller that we had seen enough and thanked him for his time and the tour. Next!

If you plan on giving tours, please remember that you are not showing them a museum. The total tour should last no more than ten to fifteen minutes, with added time for the buyers to walk around the house again for a second look. If you are thinking of going the FSBO route, it may take a while longer to sell and you and the buyers will most certainly run into some sort of issues. Even with real estate agents on both sides of a transaction, it can get heated and close to coming unglued due to the demands of both sides.

After the home inspection, buyers will think the home is way worse than they'd previously imagined and sellers will feel insulted that the sentimental home they've lived in for so long is being denigrated by the buyers. Lastly, the longer it sits for sale, the better the chance of having your home stigmatized with buyers thinking *What's wrong with this house?*

Most agents have experience dealing with all of this on a regular basis and are used to problem-solving and know good, reliable contractors who can assist, since many problems between the buyer and seller are due to home inspection issues and are often repair related. In fact, the most common reason for a home sale to fall through is due to issues brought up in the home inspection.

The second biggest reason is due to the inability of the buyer to obtain financing.

I've already given you my personal take on the benefits of using a professional real estate agent and we will discuss some other items about which you may not even have thought. Even though I am a licensed Realtor® and broker, I have no problem with sellers wanting to go it alone. I have worked with *for sale by owners* in the past and have sold their properties by introducing them to interested buyers of mine who subsequently purchased the property with my representation. The sellers agreed, in advance, to compensate me for my time and effort.

NOTE: *Real estate agents are required to undergo continuing education (CE) every couple of years. A frequent topic is the U.S. Fair Housing Laws prohibiting discrimination in housing based on race, color, religion, sex, disability, familial status, and national origin. Violations are serious and can lead to fines and severe penalties. FSBO sellers, like agents, need to be aware of these laws and abide by them.*

Tasks

The good news is you have full control over your sale and you can save a lot of money. You dictate exactly at what amount you will list the home and are in command of all of the terms. However, you will also be responsible for all of your own marketing and for acquiring all of the necessary real estate documents. You will also be in charge of receiving all the phone calls, stray door knockers and conducting all tours. If everything goes well, you will then be in charge of reviewing purchase offers to include determining the financial wherewithal of the purchaser's ability to obtain financing. See Chapter 20 for information on the different types of financing that can make or break your deal.

You'll be responsible for the timing of all the different home inspections and will need to be home to let everyone inside. You will also be dealing with the home inspection request for repairs and determining what is fair and more in tune with the agreement of sale and which items are overkill. Home inspection negotiations typically take between five days to a week to finalize.

You will then be in charge of getting all of the repair estimates and coordinate the work to ensure everything is completed in time for settlement. You will also need to assemble all the repair receipts to be given to the buyers prior to their final walkthrough. If all of that is completed satisfactory, you must be available to allow the appraiser access to the property to do their review. You will be notified if the appraisal comes in below the purchase price and you will want to figure out how you can fight this low appraisal and attempt to get it corrected. See Chapter 22 for detailed information on the appraisal process.

Depending upon the type of financing utilized, the lender may inform you of specifically needed repairs noted by the appraiser and will send you the applicable portion of the appraiser's report for review. They will then follow up with you to see if the repairs have been finished. If so, another appointment time will be arranged to confirm the repairs. If not, you will need to complete the work in time, or settlement will be delayed. I've seen cases where the work is complete and pictures have been taken as proof, but the appraiser is unable to get to the property on time to confirm the repairs, so the settlement is postponed until the work is verified, as the lender won't move forward even with photos showing the work has been performed.

You will also want to keep track of the
mortgage commitment. The due date should have been
written into the contract. This is a measuring stick to make
sure the lender has done most of their due diligence and that
they will commit to the loan. There are usually some added
clauses to the commitment, such as *buyer needs to retain x-
amount of funds in their bank account,* or *purchase is
contingent upon the buyer's final credit review,* etc. I like to
call the lender and talk directly with them so I can get a
better feel for the commitment and how thorough it is. I've
seen some that have had so many additional contingencies,
such as satisfactory appraisal, along with a host of other
issues, that it makes the document practically worthless.

If the closing date is looking iffy, I want to be able to
notify my seller so that they can make necessary
arrangements on their end, should things not go as planned.
There's nothing worse than finding out the day of settlement
that you won't be closing due to lender issues. Best to smoke
out those troubled deals ahead of time.

Once a satisfactory commitment has been presented,
it's time to start calling the utility company about having your
service transferred into the buyer's name on the day of the
closing. You will also want to contact your
internet provider/cable company, along with your
trash hauler, if you do not have municipal waste collection.
You may need to contact the water company if the closing
agent is not going to do so.

Hopefully things are going smoothly at your next
destination and you can finalize packing things and
preparing for the movers. These are stressful times, so don't
blame yourself if you feel like punching something. It's a
great time to get in some exercise and blow off steam. My

motto is to *keep your eye on the prize*, meaning don't forget why you are doing this and keep the end goal in mind. Don't just focus on the seemingly never-ending drudgery.

You will need to set up a date with the purchaser to have their final walkthrough, where they will be reviewing the property to make sure it is in the same condition as when they wrote their offer, double-check that any home repairs have been completed and make sure the inclusions are still in the home.

TIP: Some attorneys in non-attorney states will settle the real estate transaction for the same cost as a title company. This gives the buyer the added oversight of having an attorney answer their many questions. I highly recommend this to buyers and sellers, since it can make for a smoother transaction.

Lastly, you should contact the buyer's lender and make sure they have been cleared to close. It's also a good idea to contact the closing agent to ask for a copy of the closing disclosure that breaks down all of your expenses and credits along with your final mortgage payout.

On the day of settlement, you should remember to bring any extra keys, garage door remotes, codes to external garage door openers, etc. Buyers will appreciate you not forgetting these items and for not having to receive them by mail at a later date. If you happen to get the buyer from h*ll, he or she may even want you to escrow funds until they receive the items that you forgot. Don't give them the chance. Make a note to bring these items and put them somewhere safe (like in your car) where you know you will be able to find them.

TIP: *It's a nice gesture for the sellers to provide the buyers with all warranty info, owner's manuals, blueprints and whatever other household literature you have that you won't be using anymore. This is invaluable to a purchaser who may not even know how to properly operate some of your systems such as the house alarm. Such niceties can go a long way and lead to a smoother settlement with fewer disruptions about minuscule issues.*

Once all the documents are signed and the lender has approved the signed contracts, the keys are given to the buyers and the checks are dispersed. All parties (hopefully) shake hands and walk away feeling great that everything went well and they got what they wanted. You walk away convinced that you maximized your profit in the least amount of time and inconvenience. The buyer walks away knowing they purchased the right house.

These are the many tasks that a FSBO will need to undertake on their own. As you can see, there are lots of balls in the air that need to be accounted for at all times. You will also need to keep track of the specific dates that each task is to be completed since most contracts state that *time is of the essence,* meaning dates need to be followed. Otherwise, they must be changed and agreed to by all parties prior to the date's arrival. If all of this sounds intimidating, you should contact a real estate agent and review their qualifications to see how they can best assist you.

Safety

You need to remember that if you go this route, you will be inviting complete strangers into your home with you as their guide. Sometimes it will be only one or two people. Other times it could be five or six. Of the two brokers I have worked with as an independent contractor, both of them held occasional group safety meetings. Safety is paramount, especially if there are little ones in the house.

The sad truth is that there have been multiple real estate agents killed during the course of their day to day work. It is a dark topic which I would prefer not to discuss, but it is a reality in today's world. Just recently a female agent was attacked at an open house she was holding for her sellers. The incident was captured on a *Ring* doorbell camera, which provided good evidence to the police. It's disturbing that the camera's presence didn't deter the perpetrator from attacking her in the first place, which shows the total lack of sense the perpetrator displayed.

Although there are things that can be done to better protect you, it's hard to defend yourself from an attack without any kind of warning. I have learned from prior safety training not too let unknown prospects walk directly behind you and to keep them in your field of vision at all times. If there are more than one, let them know they should stay together and not wander off. It's a good idea to let friends or loved ones check in with you afterward to make sure everything went smoothly. It is also a good idea to inform the buyers that you are in constant contact with friends or other family members. A good way to do this is to call someone right after they arrive and say something like,

"Wanted to let you know the buyers just arrived, I'll call you back once they have left."

Although it can be fun to meet strangers, it can also be a little nerve-racking, especially at night. Make sure you have a *Plan B* should things go awry. If you are overly concerned about having unknown visitors enter your home, you can always say something like the following when they arrive: "You look like really nice people, but you can never be too careful these days. I just want to let you know in advance that we have security cameras located throughout the house. I hope you don't mind." Most likely, the buyers won't care. If it is a problem, I suggest you end the meeting. The tour is now over. Be sure to read Chapter 15, Personal and Home Security, for more in-depth safety tips for you and your family.

If you are going to sell FSBO, you should consider working with buyer's agents and offer to pay out a fair commission in order to get maximum activity on your home. You will be saving lots of money by not having to pay a commission to a listing agent. Some agents won't work with FSBO's, but others will be happy to show and sell your property, provided they are adequately compensated for their time and effort.

Keep in mind that agents will most likely not be working for you, but for their buyer clients, and will be acting in their best interests. Be sure to review the agency laws in your particular area to determine how they are structured. See Chapter 9 for additional information on Agency Relationships. The money you are saving by not paying a listing agent also means you will forgo exclusive seller representation along with a lack of fiduciary, or special trust and confidence when dealing directly with a buyer's agent. Thus, the buyer's agent is not acting on your behalf and will be trying to negotiate terms more advantageous to the buyer.

Keep in mind, the buyer's agent probably knows much more about transacting real estate than you do, even though it is your home that is being sold. Make sure the money you are saving does not cost you even more money in excess home repairs and other concessions in the long run.

Going it alone can be a very rewarding experience if everything goes as planned. If you choose this route, you will want a team of professionals including an attorney, contractors, and movers ready to help facilitate the process. Should you decide to hire a real estate agent, most of them will already have a core group of professionals prepared to assist you when needed.

In the following chapter, I will provide you with important qualifications to look for when choosing a real estate agent. I will also explain the difference between a Realtor® and a real estate agent and provide you with questions to ask your potential hires when conducting interviews. Grab your clipboard and let's get started!

Chapter 9

Hiring an Agent

"It doesn't make sense to hire smart people and then tell them what to do;
we hire smart people so they can tell us what to do."
~Steve Jobs

Unless you live in a rural part of the country, you are probably surrounded by lots of real estate agents. So much so, that you couldn't throw a lovesick cat without hitting a couple of them. Where I live in the mid-Atlantic there is fierce competition for buyers and listings, so consumers get the pick of the litter.

Just because there is more of something doesn't mean that it's any easier to choose. In fact, sometimes it makes it more difficult to make the best selection. Think about the last time you went into a big box store and wanted to purchase something simple like work gloves, and you were faced with choosing between 25 pairs ranging from mechanic gloves to garden gloves, cleaning gloves, heavy-duty gloves, leather gloves, canvas gloves, rubber gloves, neoprene gloves, etc. There are so many different kinds that you may have walked out of the store with nothing but a headache. Sometimes you actually wish there were fewer choices so you could easily pick one and be off to the next task on your to-do list.

You are most likely bombarded with real estate postcards, emails, newsletters, commercials, radio ads, TV ads, flyers, door hangers, etc., with all of them pitching generally the same thing. *Pick me to buy or sell a home.* Or, *Come look at my just-listed property.* Or, *Look at me, I sold 123 Main Street!*

With so many choices it's tough to know where to begin. I am going to break it down for you and provide you with some basic tips for finding a real estate agent who is a good fit for you. Be sure to review the last section of this chapter for some specific questions to ask potential agents.

There are several different topics we're going to be looking at. I will break them down for you and touch on them in depth later in the chapter.

They are:

> - Realtor® versus Real Estate Agent
> - Agency Relationships
> - Knowledge of the Area
> - Experience
> - Accountability and Work Habits
> - Communications and Technology
> - Marketing
> - Personality and Character
> - Individual Agents versus Teams
> - Questions to Ask

Realtor® versus Real Estate Agent

Do you know the difference between a Realtor® and a real estate agent? If you are thinking one is licensed and the other is not you would be incorrect. The difference is as follows: A Realtor® is a licensed real estate agent in their state, and a member of the National Association of Realtors® (NAR) and is consequently bound by their Standards of Practice. There are 17 articles in the Standards of Practice. For example, Article 1 states that when dealing with buyers, sellers, etc., the Realtor® will protect and uphold the interests of their client and treat all "parties honestly."[1]

Real estate agents are licensed in the state in which they work, but they are not all members of the National Association of Realtors®. In short, Realtors® are bound by the NAR Code of Ethics along with the laws in the state in which they are licensed. Real estate agents are merely bound by the laws of the state in which they practice, which can be vague in terms of fairness to clients and other agents. Realtors® go the extra mile that real estate agents don't necessarily subscribe to.

It's important that rules are followed for the benefit of everyone and for the protection of the public. Without the NAR, many unfair practices would be commonplace. The NAR also serves as a consumer advocate by lobbying for issues such as preserving first time-buyer incentives, along with efforts to maintain low transfer taxes, etc.

---

[1] "Copyright 2020 NATIONAL ASSOCIATION OF REALTORS®. Reprinted with permission."

Agency Relationships

State laws vary regarding agency and agency relationships. The bottom line is that you want your agent to owe his or her fiduciary duties to you as your listing agent and represent your best interests at all times. However, if your agent procures the buyer, chances are your agent is going to be a dual agent, meaning he or she is representing both parties equally but cannot disclose confidential information about one party to the other.

For example, real estate agent Joe Sellit works for Get-It-Done Real Estate. Joe has just found a buyer for his sellers' property. The buyer is also Joe's client and he will be earning both sides of the commission. Both clients must consent to dual agency or else other arrangements will need to be made in order to finalize the transaction, such as the buyer chooses to work with a different agent.

Whenever a listing agent and buyer's agent work for the same company, it means the broker also becomes a dual agency since they are representing both agent's clients. This can actually work to your advantage should the deal start to fall apart, because the broker may be more willing to keep the deal together in order to avoid losing both sides of the transaction. Most brokers remain at arm's length for many transactions unless there is a problem that is directly brought to their attention. I personally don't see a dual agency broker being detrimental to a transaction.

TIP: *Some states don't allow dual agency relationships. Speak to a local real estate professional, or real estate attorney to see what the current laws are in your state.*

I also don't have a problem with one agent representing both clients, as long as both parties agree to it in writing and the agent has a solid real estate background along with a successful track record. I have done transactions as a dual agent and all of them went smoothly. The bottom line is to make sure you know who your agent represents at all times. Your listing agreement should spell out, in detail, the different types of relationships available to you.

Knowledge of the Area

I can move to your state tomorrow, and get a real estate license, sign on with a broker, and be up and selling real estate in minimal time. Should I be your top choice for listing your home, knowing that I have been in the area for less than 30 days? Although I possess many of the other aforementioned qualities, I am not as familiar with your area as you are. Of course, I can and will learn over time, but that takes a while. For example, there are developments in my area which are across the street from one another and yet one of them sells for approximately 10 to 15% more than the other. How would an agent new to the area know about this?

Agents with a history of working in your area should have good knowledge about it, such as which roads to take during rush hour, along with the advantages and disadvantages of all the different neighborhoods to live in. An experienced local agent should be more effective in selling your property because of their greater knowledge of the market along with a more accurate pulse of the surrounding area and is best suited to obtain the maximum sales price.

In short, there is definite value in hiring an agent with extensive knowledge of your area. Your listing agent will be able to inform buyers of where the local attractions and best shopping are, where the schools are located and can provide valuable knowledge to a prospective buyer to help sell your home. Knowledge of the area is an important criterion when choosing an agent.

Experience

If you were having major surgery next week, would you feel comfortable if this was your surgeon's first operation? Or would you feel more confident knowing he or she has done these dozens or even hundreds of times? Of course, you would want the experienced surgeon who knows his or her way around the block, or your body, for that matter. Now the question becomes-how much experience?

There are no hard and fast rules for this question, but seasoned agents know where the booby traps are and can safely navigate around them. How do we know this? Because we've walked into them many years ago and learned the hard way.

If you are using an inexperienced agent to sell the most expensive asset you have ever owned, do you want them to be discovering some of these minefields during your listing? The following is an example of one such trap I encountered in my early days as a Realtor®. I had successfully gotten one of my first listings under contract and we were now at the settlement table signing documents. I was seated next to my seller client, and the buyers and their agent were across the table from us. All of a sudden the seller says to me out loud, "How much money am I getting back for the oil that is leftover in my tank?"

Since I was brand new, I didn't know I was responsible for notifying my seller about getting the oil tank dipped by their provider in order to determine how much oil was left in the tank and what the current value was to be paid to the seller at closing. Depending upon where you live and what the current price of heating oil is, this amount may exceed $750. I asked the seller how much oil he thought he had in the tank and he said, "Probably around 100 gallons." A quick search of the going rate found that it was approximately $3.25 per gallon, which would total $325 dollars. I asked the buyer's agent if the buyer would be willing to cut a check to the seller for this amount.

Thankfully, the buyer was a very nice person and he understood the dilemma and was happy to make it right. *Whewwww.* This is a classic example of a real estate snafu lying in wait for newer agents. There are dozens of similar types of traps lurking out there for unsuspecting agents to obliviously step into. If you want to lessen your chances of blunders during your sale, then you should seriously consider hiring an agent with a good amount of experience in real estate sales.

Accountability and Work Habits

It's possible you will find a qualified real estate agent with a wonderful knowledge of the area and lots of experience, but who still may not be a good fit for you. I have seen agents hold second jobs and be unavailable to their clients when important issues arise that demand immediate attention. For example, suppose you've just listed your home with a local agent named Billy Jones of Sell-it-Fast Real Estate. John Smith, a buyer's agent, wants to write an offer on your property and has some important questions to which the buyers need answers before writing their offer. Since the buyers are flying home this evening, it's imperative that Billy respond to their requests ASAP.

Unfortunately, all texts and voicemails go unanswered for hours on end because Billy is working his other job as a paramedic. Since John Smith can't get a hold of your agent with the buyer's questions and concerns, the buyers start to feel as if they are being slighted because of a lack of a response. They assume this is a sign that it's just not the right house for them and decide to forgo writing an offer and keep looking. They may also think that if the sellers are this slow to respond before getting a contract, they may be difficult to work with. Unfortunately, the sellers had nothing to do with this communication breakdown but bore the brunt of its consequences thanks to their inattentive agent.

These scenarios happen, as buyers can become superstitious when making the biggest purchase of their lives. You want an agent who will be accountable much of the day. If they do hold a second job, it's important that they have another agent covering for them while they are indisposed. It is inexcusable for a client or another agent to not be able to reach your agent for long periods of time.

I have done many deals with *out to lunch* agents like this and they can really make us look bad. I end up doing many of the duties myself. I have even seen some listing agents not provide any photographs for their listing. These

CHAPTER 9 HIRING AN AGENT | 89

are typically the same agents who don't stipulate any room measurements in the MLS property description sheets because it's just too much trouble for them. Steer clear of these types by asking to see prior MLS property descriptions on homes they have sold. This will give you an upfront indicator as to the quality of their work.

If I am working with a seller and receive two identical purchase offers, one from a less competent agent and the other from an easy to reach, hard working full-time agent, I will let the seller know that the former agent is not very accountable and is difficult to deal with and recommend they seriously consider the other offer. You may never know that your agent is not doing their job, so good work habits and accountability are very important factors you should consider when hiring a real estate professional.

Communications and Technology

Some of this overlaps the prior lesson but contains some important distinctions worth noting. You may have an agent who is accountable and who has good work habits but is not very proficient with all the different levels of work communications. For example, many times clients will have to travel for work and might be personally unavailable. However, when transacting real estate, there are deadlines that must be met as the show must go on whether they are in town or not. Most contracts will state that *time is of the essence*, and it's important to operate within the agreed-upon dates.

If my clients need to respond to a document in writing, it may be difficult for them to do so, which is why I subscribe to a program called DocuSign, where I can send my clients documents via email and they can easily sign them from their computer or smartphone. This way, there are no delays and the deadlines can be achieved regardless of where my client is in the world. Missing deadlines is a good way to lose leverage in a deal or have it fall apart entirely. It's important to follow the rules of the contract and abide by them.

There are lots of moving parts in a transaction, and when agents are conducting multiple deals at the same time it is easy for something important to fall through the cracks. It is not possible for a busy real estate agent to conduct business without the aid of proficient real estate software that keeps track of every detail of every sale. I use a professional real estate program and database which keeps track of everything, sending me notices of when a deadline is due. It also tracks all of the 45+ activities that need to take place in any one transaction. Without it, I would be rummaging through manilla folders all day long trying to coordinate transactions manually.

If your agent is traveling and does not have another agent covering for them, will they be able to effectively work your transaction away from the office? Make sure they can, because your deal depends upon them being accessible when away. Communications both in writing and verbally, along with advanced knowledge of technology, is vital. Make sure your agent is well versed in this.

It's important that your agent or the broker for which they work have a robust website that allows purchasers to search all of the area listings. My current website allows buyers to see all of our property listings, conduct online market analyses, get important area and school information, along with lots of other data. The more buyers who visit the site, the better the chance they have of viewing our inventory and wanting to tour the homes.

Finally, your agent should be able to produce professional photos of your property in order for it to look its best and entice buyers to want to tour the home. Personally, I feel professional photographers do this best, which is why I provide this service to my clients. Poor photographs can make a property appear undesirable and not worthy of a buyer's visit.

TIP: *Be sure to ask for references from the agent you are considering so you can contact some of their former clients for an endorsement of their work.*

Marketing

It goes without saying that marketing is an important component in selling your home. If no one is aware your house is for sale, it doesn't matter how wonderful it is, because it can't sell if no one knows about it. You want to choose an agent that will take full advantage of the many different marketing opportunities available. Due to the importance of this topic, I devoted an entire chapter to it. Because of this, I will briefly review the areas of marketing and explain them in greater detail in Chapter 15.

Your agent should be able to provide you with a colorful real estate sign along with a dedicated webpage with your home's listing information. You also want to see your property listed in the MLS and all of the top third-party real estate sites that I review in-depth in Chapter 11. The agent

you choose should have a good online social presence and
be able to market your property on all the various social
media sites. It also never hurts to have some print advertising
utilizing postcards to get the word out. Lastly, they should be
willing to hold an *open house* at your request.

Personality and Character

It's very important that you and your chosen real estate
professional get along well and are able to easily talk about
difficult issues. It's vital that you feel comfortable
communicating with him or her and are not intimidated by
your agent.

For example, have you ever been on a medical
appointment and felt rushed and intimidated by the doctor?
You didn't get to ask all of the questions that you wanted to
be answered? I think we all can relate to this and can agree
that your questions are important, and you should have the
confidence that your real estate professional will take the
time to review the process, address all your concerns and not
make you feel rushed.

It is also vital that you align yourself with someone
who shares your general principals of honesty and integrity.
It wouldn't hurt to do some online research on your
candidate to see what others are saying and if they have been
mentioned in any news articles. You can also check with the
Better Business Bureau to see if they or their broker has had
any complaints.

Does your candidate support the local community by
giving back? Do they partake in programs that help out
people who can't purchase homes without assistance, such as

Habitat for Humanity? Obviously, you don't want them spending the bulk of their time with charitable organizations. However, there appears to be a direct correlation between charitable, giving people and the hardworking and honorable folks with whom you should consider working. Integrity and character should be of utmost importance in selecting an agent.

TIP: *"Buying the listing" is when a potential listing agent tells homeowners that their property can be priced higher than it should and higher than other competing agents have suggested. They do this because many homeowners believe they can sell their home for more than it's actually worth, so they choose the agent who quotes a price they like instead of the one that's realistic. Once the agent lists your property, they will push for frequent price reductions because they know it is priced too high. Be wary of agents who promise you an unrealistic sales price. Make sure the comparable sold properties justify the price at which you choose to list. Too high of a listing price can lead to longer days on the market, which can negatively affect your actual selling price.*

Individual Agents versus Teams

Many people seem to be in awe of how much business a team can perform, without stopping to think about what it really means. For example, Daffy Keys works for PDQ Real Estate and has a team of 25 agents working for her in which all of their sales count towards Team Daffy's total sales. If each of the 25 agents complete 14 deals a year averaging $300,000 per transaction, it means Team Daffy produced

$105 million dollars in sales that year (25 agents x 14 deals x $300,000 per deal = $105 million). This gives you the impression that Team Daffy is absolutely amazing because their production is so high. However, it only thrives because there are so many agents involved with transacting business, which is why their total sales number is so large. In essence, they are a small company (Team Daffy), within a larger company (PDQ Real Estate).

This doesn't mean that Daffy, the team founder, is super-human or more knowledgeable than any of the other agents on the team. It simply means Daffy has set up a wholesale operation, geared for volume. Volume should have nothing to do with your home, since your home is not a commodity, nor should it be treated as one.

In fact, when working with a team, you are more apt to work with different people within the team. For example, Mary Lock is selling 123 Main Street and has a representative from Team Daffy to list her home. This would typically be one of their better, more personable agents who will be focused on getting the listing. Once the listing is procured, Mary may find herself dealing with another team member who is focused primarily on listing inventory and marketing. Once the house goes under contract, Mary may then be handed to yet a different team member who specializes in closing transactions.

When it's all said and done, Mary could have worked with as many as two or three different team members with just the one transaction. Mary may find herself repeating her wishes and concerns over and over again to different members of the team in order to bring each one of them up to speed on her situation.

In comparison, when you work with one agent, you get individualized attention every step of the way. You get one phone number and one email address to reach out to. There is no getting reacquainted with other people during the sale. Let's face it. Would you rather work with your doctor or work with the doctor's assistant's assistant? You should consider working with someone with the most experience, who is knowledgeable in all aspects of the transaction and not just an assembly line agent performing for a team.

Talk with both and see which you feel more comfortable with. It's imperative that you and your home are of the utmost importance to the agent and not just another address.

Questions to Ask

- **How long have you been selling real estate in this area?**
  <u>Response:</u> You are looking for at least three-to-five years. The more experienced, the better.
- **Where do you live and what specific territory do you most like to work?**
  <u>Response:</u> You want them to specialize in your area and not live far away. You are less likely to see them if they live farther away.
- **Are you full time, or do you have any other responsibilities?**
  <u>Response:</u> You are looking for a full-time real estate commitment with minimal other responsibilities.

- **Are you a member of the National Association of Realtors®?**
  Response: Yes. Realtors® subscribe to a strict code of ethics.

- **How many total real estate transactions have you done?**
  Response: Look for a minimum of 50 transactions.

- **What is your marketing plan?**
  Response: (See Marketing section in this chapter.)

- **Why should I hire you?**
  Response: You want to feel comfortable in knowing they are honest, a good fit, that they will be responsive to your calls and emails and you generally feel they will be able to sell your home in the shortest amount of time for the most money.

- **How long do I have to list my home with you?**
  Response: At least three months, no longer than six months in a good market.

- **What is your total commission and what percentage do you give to the buyer's agent?**
  Response: Commission rates are negotiable. The buyer's agent's commission should be customary for your area.

- **How will you contact me and how often?**
  Response: The types of communications are your personal preference. Frequency should be a least once a week.

- **How often do you go away or take vacations? Do you have someone to cover for you when you're away?**

Response: You want to make sure they are working during your peak season. The fewer the vacations the better. You need to know if someone will be taking over when they're away.

- **Are you part of a team or do you work with assistants?**
  Response: If the agent has lots of assistants or works with a team, you may not have many interactions with the agent you are currently interviewing.

- **Do you hold a salesperson's license or a broker's license?**
  Response: Obtaining a broker's license requires additional education and training and shows a dedication to the business.

Choosing the right agent should take into careful consideration the many different qualities that make up the ideal candidate for you. Don't leave it to chance to determine who you will be working with. Do your homework and get it right the first time.

In the next chapter, I will pull back the curtain and discuss the truth about real estate commissions. There are lots of misconceptions regarding this topic, so grab your calculator and let's dive in!

Chapter 10

The Truth About
Commissions and Contracts

"If you pay peanuts, you get monkeys."
~Chinese Proverb

There appears to be many misnomers and
misconceptions about real estate commissions. Who pays
the buyer's agent? Why does one company cost more than
another? Is a broker's commission negotiable?

Commissions are paid by the seller at an amount that
was agreed upon when the property was listed for sale with a
real estate agent. Buyers are typically not responsible for
paying commissions on a transaction. The listing agreement
will spell out in detail exactly what percentage of the
purchase price will be paid as commission to the procuring
agent at the time of settlement. It will also specify how much
of the collected commission will be given to the buyer's
agent who brings the winning offer. The buyer's agent

commission amount is written in the MLS property description for all real estate agents to see. For example, Charles Gaines lists his house at 105 Ormond Road with Doug Campbell, an agent with Sell-it-Now Real Estate. The total commission on the listing agreement is 6% of the purchase price. Half of that amount, or 3%, will be stated in the MLS and paid to the agent's broker who brings the successful buyer. Mr. Gaines pays no up-front monies to the listing agent or the agent's broker, and he allows them six months to market and sell the property. If they are unsuccessful, he can renew his agreement or cancel it and list the home with someone else. Unless stated otherwise, he will owe the agent and broker no money if the house does not sell.

Antitrust Laws

Price fixing falls under the Federal anti-trust act and is in place to keep fair competition and prevent collusion. For example, what if there were only four real estate companies in the town of Potterville and the CEOs of each company got together to discuss and agree that they will all charge no less than 8% commission on every transaction. This way there would be no discounted rates and the four companies will compete with each other in other ways, such as experience and service. How does that sound? Certainly not good for the consumers in Potterville, but pretty darn good for the four real estate companies, since their minimum commission is now 8%. This is a good example of price-fixing and what a disadvantage it is for consumers.

However, there is a caveat. Not all brokerages can afford to conduct a *bare-bones* operation and charge low commissions. Some brokerages have higher than average costs such as rental space, parking, insurance, and staff, in addition to their typical expenses such as telephones, MLS dues, utilities, computers, desks, office supplies, etc.

All companies need to make a profit in order to stay in business. Just because ABC Real Estate can sell your home for 5.0% commission, does not mean that PDQ Real Estate can do the same. Some real estate companies may have bare minimums they cannot go below according to company policy.

To break it down even further, all commissions go to the broker of record, for example, ABC Real Estate. Realtors® and real estate agents cannot conduct business without having their license affiliated with a real estate broker, meaning when you obtain your real estate license, you cannot conduct business until you are signed up by a broker. The real estate broker acts as a governing body to oversee the agent's actions and keep the agent in line with the current rules and regulations in their particular area.

Brokers and agents have their own agreements as to what percentage of the pie the agent will get for each transaction. With newer recruits, the split is typically 50%. Seasoned agents have a higher split, which can reach as high as 90% to the agent and 10% to the broker. Much of this depends upon how much business the agent does. This is an advantage of teams, in which the leader of the team can negotiate a better split due to the increased sales volume.

Real estate agents also have many fees to pay, including errors and omissions insurance (E&O), licensing fees, continuing education fees, MLS fees, board dues, gasoline and car expenses, cell phone costs, advertising, signs, etc. Agents also need to turn a profit or they will not be able to pay their bills. It's important to note that real estate agents are not employees of the brokers they work for, but are classified as *independent contractors*, which means they don't receive salaries or benefits and have totally different responsibilities and duties than employees do.

Because real estate agents work only on commission, if they do not sell a property, they do not get paid for their services. They also have totally different responsibilities and duties than employees do. For example, their broker cannot tell them when to come to work, or how long they must stay. They also can't require them to attend regular meetings. Since they are not employees, they aren't subjected to the same scrutiny that a typical employee would be.

Discount Commissions

If you do happen to find a broker that is willing to accept very low commissions, there are some very important drawbacks to consider. In selling your home, you pay a percentage of the real estate commission to your listing broker and the other percentage to the selling broker, aka the buyer's broker. In most cases, this percentage will be 50/50, but it is very important that you find out the precise percentage. You need to be aware of what percentage you are paying out to the buyer's broker, as it may be less than you thought. For example, let's say in Mayberry County, Gregg Brady of PDQ Realty offers you a low commission of 4.5% to list your house. You agree in writing that PDQ Realty will be paying out 1.5% of the 4.5% to whichever agent's brokerage brings the successful buyer. This means that Greg and PDQ Realty will be keeping the lion's share of the commission, which is 3%.

However, it turns out that the average buyer's broker commission in Mayberry County is 3%, meaning, a buyer's agent is looking to tour buyers throughout Mayberry County and all of the homes listed for sale are paying 3% to buyers' brokers, while your house is only paying 1.5%. Which homes do you think the buyer's agent is going to show first? You're correct if you said, "Not mine." Do you think the savings in commission could end up costing you more money in the long run? It sure could, especially if your house ends up sitting on the market for a while. I know seasoned agents who wouldn't show your house if it was the last home on the market because you are paying too low of a commission. There are better ways to expose your property to the most qualified buyers and their agents.

Think about your own job. If you are given the choice of doing Project A that will pay you $5,000 or Project B that will take the same amount of time and effort, but only pays you $3,000, which one are you going to be motivated to work on? Now, imagine that you are faced with this decision every month of your career. Do you think you will really ever want to consider Project B? This is the reality of paying out a low buyer's agent compensation. Homes that pay higher commissions typically get shown first. When buyers find a house they like, they attempt to purchase it and no longer look at other homes for sale. So, the first homes shown are likely to sell faster than homes that are shown last.

The shorter the amount of time your home sits on the market, the more money you will make. Consequently, the longer it sits on the market, the less money it will bring in. Buyers love it when they find out that a house they are interested in has been on the market for a long time, because they know they can lowball their offer and have a better chance of getting it accepted, verses lowballing a newly listed property. In fact, one of the first questions I get asked when touring a buyer through a property in which they are interested in, "How long has it been on the market?" If the answer is, "A few days," they know they need to act fast and present a strong offer. On the other hand, if the answer is, "It has been on the market for 165 days," then they will be discussing how they can get the property for cheap.

We live in a capitalist society where income is vitally important to our existence and the natural human instinct is to get as much as we can for the same amount of work. Does this mean your home won't be shown? Of course not. There are agents like me who will let their buyer clients decide which properties they want to see, and the commission will be an afterthought. However, what I am saying is that you will most likely get fewer agents showing your home because you are paying so little in commission.

When I was in college working my summer job at a local restaurant, there was a regular customer who came in practically every night that would never tip his waiters or waitresses. He would always leave a note stating *It is the owner's responsibility to pay you fair wages and I won't be the one to compensate you for your time and service.*

How do you think that went over with the waitstaff? Every night I would hear them moan and complain that they got the cheapskate at their table and what a son of a b*tch he was for not tipping. He was not leaving them a customary amount like the other patrons were and the waitstaff was really upset about it. I know he did not receive great service and Lord knows what they did to his food.

Of course, customers are not obliged to tip, with the exception of large parties. However, there is an expectation and if that expectation is not met, it creates negative feelings and can result in unintended consequences. So, things may not turn out the way you expected them to if you are not paying a fair and customary amount.

For example, is the agent to whom you are paying so little money going to do all the same things the other agent is willing to do, such as consistent marketing, open houses, premium marketing materials, maximum online exposure and being accountable every day? Are they going to be as loyal to you as they are to their clients who are paying them a higher amount?

The saying *you get what you pay for* certainly applies in real estate. You decide what you think is best given your situation. Just make sure you know how much your agent is paying out to the buyer's agent, versus how much they are keeping for themselves because it can have adverse consequences on your listing.

An investor friend of mine was trying to sell a home he had purchased and rehabbed and he was having no luck marketing it with an agent. He wanted my opinion as to why it wasn't selling. I typically don't work in the area where the house was located, but I agreed to look at it for him. After reviewing his newly fixed-up property and comparing it with similar homes that had sold, along with homes currently on the market, I discovered what the problem was. His price was spot on since the property was practically new due to all of the upgrades he had performed. I informed him that his agent was only paying out 2% to the buyer's agents and asked him what the total commission was. He said the total was 6%. Thus, the agent was keeping 4% for himself and his broker and was only paying out 2% to the buyer's agent who procured the purchaser. I enlightened him that 2% was less than the 3% that was typical in that particular area and advised him to get it corrected to the higher, customary amount.

Within a week of the commission change, he had it under contract. He had no idea his supposed *agent friend* was paying out so little in buyer's agent compensation.

Commissions play a big role in real estate sales and should be carefully evaluated. Paying a customary percentage of the sales price as commission aligns the incentives of the buyer's agent and the listing agent to make the main priority to sell your house.

Listing Contracts

There are several different types of real estate listing contracts brokers use:

- ➢ Exclusive Right to Sell Listing
- ➢ Exclusive Agency Listing
- ➢ Non-Exclusive or Open Listing

Exclusive Right to Sell Listing

This is by far the most common of all the agreements and the one I recommend. This is a written contract between the broker and property owner authorizing the broker to have the exclusive right to market and sell the owner's property during a prescribed period of time and for an agreed-upon commission.

For example, ABC Real Estate Company lists Herman Muenster's house at 1313 East Mockingbird Lane. The time period of the listing is six months and the total commission payout is 6%, half of which will be paid out to the buyer's broker side of the transaction. In short, ABC Real Estate is to receive a guaranteed 3% commission even if any other brokers introduce the buyer and write a successful purchase agreement.

ABC Real Estate has an exclusive arrangement with the seller, knowing they can spend money marketing the property with certainty they will capture a return for their efforts. Any real estate agent under any brokerage is free to show and sell the property. If an agent from ABC Real Estate also brings the successful buyer, then ABC Real Estate will retain the entire 6% commission to be split according to prior agreements with their agents. If the property does not sell within the six-month time frame, the seller can cancel the listing or renew it. Typically, the seller will owe no money if the house does not sell.

Most brokers will not consider any other type of listing agreement since this gives them peace of mind knowing that their efforts will not be in vain. It also gives the sellers access to the largest pool of buyers for increased competition to maximize their profit.

Exclusive Agency Listing

This is a contract where the owner of the property appoints one broker as their exclusive agent to sell the property. The seller retains the right to sell the property without the obligation to pay the broker a commission. Using the example above, ABC Real Estate is the only agency authorized to sell the property. However, the seller retains the right to sell the property themselves if they find a buyer on their own. Not very reassuring for the broker or their agent, who may not want to spend lots of time and effort marketing this type of listing, since they are in competition with the owner to find a buyer and may never see a return on their investment.

Exclusive agency listings provide a smaller pool of buyers for the house since it limits the number of brokers and agents who can participate in the process. Thus, competition is more limited than with an exclusive right-to-sell agreement.

Non-Exclusive or Open Listing

This is an uncommon type of listing agreement where the seller retains the right to employ any number of brokers and agents to sell the property. The brokerages can all market the property since none of them are exclusive. The seller is only obligated to pay a commission to the brokerage that brings in a successful buyer. The seller can also sell the property themselves and not be required to pay anyone a commission. Since this is viewed as a free-for-all, many brokerages won't consider this type of listing.

If you are listing your property with a brokerage, be sure to carefully review the listing agreement with your real estate agent so you fully understand the terms and conditions. If you are uncomfortable with any of the terms, be sure to have your attorney review them before you sign.

In the next chapter, I will discuss the impact third party websites play in selling your home. These sites are great at marketing properties that are for sale, but do they make it any easier for you to sell your home? Turn the page and let's find out.

Chapter 11

Third Party Real Estate Websites

"Eagles soar, but weasels
don't get sucked into jet engines."
~Steven Wright

Since the mid-2000's there has been an influx of
third-party real estate sites. Many offer free online
valuations on your home and display area houses for sale
along with the prices of sold proprieties, something that used
to be very difficult for consumers to obtain. Sites such as
*zillow.com, trulia.com, redfin.com, realtytrac.com,
homefacts.com, homefinder.com* and *homelight.com* are
just a handful of them. These sites use the Automated
Valuation Model or AVM to calculate their findings.
Computer algorithms of historical price data and pricing
trends estimate the value of the home.

If you are listing your home with a real estate agent, the agent will input your home's data into the MLS, which will cross-pollinate with most of these sites. If you are going the FSBO route, you will need to input your data on each individual site. This can be a cumbersome process since you will also want to add all of your photos.

Have you ever wondered why there are so many third-party sites? Most aren't real estate brokers but are real estate aggregators. They simply provide data but don't actually list or sell real estate. So, what is their interest in this business and why are they spending so much money on marketing their websites?

I can answer that question with two words advertising and referrals. Those third-party sites are in the business of selling advertising along with capturing actual buyers and sellers and referring them to real estate agents for a fee. Fees can be on a percentage basis, such as 25% of the gross commission earned, or it can be an agreed-upon monthly fee paid by the real estate agent each and every month.

Today many real estate agents are faced with having to pay fees and/or percentages of their commissions in order to get qualified leads that used to come from their own brokers. This is why you will see certain agents featured on some of these third-party sites. They have a financial relationship with the actual sites. Many agents find themselves having to pay these third-party sites because they are discovering it is harder to attract buyers and sellers due to so much Internet competition siphoning off customers.

Free Information

In order to attract buyers and sellers, third-party sites offer various types of free information to the public. Obviously, buyers like seeing a full display of homes for sale in their area and this is what generally attracts them. Sellers prefer to see past data on properties that have recently sold to give them an idea of what their home is worth. All they have to do is click on a link such as *what your home is worth*. They then enter an address and get a free instant evaluation.

You are probably thinking, how accurate is this valuation and how did they arrive at it? That seems to be the million-dollar question, because even they can't show you the math as to how the numbers are derived. Apparently, it all has to do with computer algorithms of large amounts of real estate data they've have compiled.

Online Valuation Comparison

If you have recently tried valuing your property, you will realize the numbers can vary greatly. For example, at the time of this writing, I plugged in the address of a local property where I grew up, to see what estimated value each site would come up with. Here are the results:

Redfin.com	$393,924
Realtytrac.com	$373,000
Zillow.com	$403,117
Homefinder.com	$363,400

*Trulia.com** $403,228

*owned by *Zillow Group Inc.*

The difference in value from the top estimate to the lowest estimate is a whopping 10%, or $39,828. A hefty sum for sure, especially if you only looked at the bottom evaluation before selling your home by owner. Of these five valuations, how many people affiliated with the above companies actually looked at the subject property in order to come up with their estimate of value? I'm guessing zero, zip and nada.

So how would they know if it has granite countertops, expensive stainless-steel appliances, imported Italian tile flooring, an exquisite Viking stove with commercial range hood, along with a state-of-the-art heating and air conditioning system? The answer is, they wouldn't. It could have the original Formica countertops, vinyl flooring, yellow-colored appliances, and single-pane windows and it would get the same evaluation. Why? Because they are not estimating the home's value on its specific improvements in comparison with other area homes.

So, if you own the lavish property I described in the former example, you are feeling pretty awful about now. But if you own the tired, original equipment home, you're feeling pretty darned good because you didn't spend a nickel to improve your property and yet it's lumped in the same value as the lavish home. The good news for the lavish home is these estimations are not current standards of practice for establishing value in residential real estate. They are merely computer-derived computations.

This is why in-person appraisals are necessary, even if they are not perfect since they can identify specific qualities one house has that another does not. Interestingly, I have heard that lenders are liking the idea of spending less money and time on appraisals and are interested in incorporating computer algorithms for establishing value. The obvious problem is the inaccuracy of the data. If this can be remedied to where the findings are more precise, it may eventually become commonplace in certain types of appraisals.

If you do visit one or all of these third-party sites, you will find the numbers are not the same unless two of the sites are owned by the same company. Do not consider any of these values to be gospel without having a comparative market analysis (CMA) done by a real estate agent or having your home appraised by a licensed appraiser who actually visits your home. Remember the phrase *"garbage in, garbage out?"* If the information going in is inaccurate then the results can also be inaccurate. At best, the sites offer real estate data such as active and sold homes; however, it is difficult to distinguish important details of the sold properties in order to paint a more vivid picture for comparison purposes.

Third-party websites can give you a ballpark idea as to how many zeros your sales price should contain; however, you will want to fine-tune that amount with some professional guidance, so you don't end up shortchanging yourself.

In the next chapter, I will review how to price your home so you can maximize its value. The right starting price can determine how successful your sale will be. There are many different schools of thought, so grab a quick snack and let's get started.

PART IV:
DUE DILIGENCE

Chapter 12

Pricing Your Home

"Price is what you pay, value is what you get."
~Warren Buffet

There are many different schools of thought when it comes to pricing your home. Real estate agents may come up with one value and licensed appraisers may come up with another. Appraisers can give the impression that home appraisals are to some extent an exact science; however, there is far too much subjectivity for this to be accurate.

For example, early in my real estate days I frequently did business with a relocation company that handled many home purchases and sales for DuPont employees. As a service to them, DuPont would buy out their existing home and then have a relocation company sell the property via a real estate broker. This would alleviate their employees from having to worry about selling their properties and it would provide them with a known selling value so they could adequately plan for their future purchase in a new area.

Appraisals

To start the sales process, real estate agents were required to get two licensed appraisers to appraise the home. If the appraisals differed by more than 5%, they were required to get a third appraisal done to get a better handle on the home's value. More times than not, a third appraisal was needed, since the first two differed by more than 5%.

Which begs the question, why was there so much price discrepancy on the same house, at the same time of year, under the same economic conditions? You may be thinking that 5% isn't much of a difference. Let's say the first appraisal valued the home at $400,000 and the second appraiser valued it at $430,000. The percentage difference in the example is 7.2%. This percentage may not seem like a lot, but it does amount to $30,000, which is a hefty sum. If this example was a DuPont relocation, it would require a third appraisal to hopefully narrow the range to a closer value.

In my opinion, the reason the numbers were often dissimilar is because residential real estate appraisals are subject to speculation and diverse opinions by the different appraisers. To get a better understanding of this, I will briefly explain to you how appraisers conduct their business and derive the numbers they do.

A fee appraisal is done by an independent, licensed or certified real estate appraiser who has no biases towards the property, meaning they have no affiliation or business interests with the homeowner, purchaser or the property itself. For example, if your sister is a licensed or certified appraiser, she should not be doing the fee appraisal on your home because she has a conflict of interest (either good or bad depending upon your relationship) because she is your sister.

The appraiser will compare similar homes and add and subtract specific dollar amounts depending upon the square footage and particular features of the home. Once all of this has been completed, the appraiser will assign a value to the property. It is a painstakingly tedious task comparing several different properties' characteristics in this manner.

Comparative Market Analysis - CMA

A real estate comparative market analysis is an evaluation conducted by a licensed real estate agent to determine what the likely sales amount will be if the house is put on the market for sale at a given time. Real estate agents use this as their primary tool for determining what they believe a house will sell for. This analysis is not an official appraisal because it is not performed by a licensed or certified appraiser.

Real estate market analyses may also vary because real estate agents have differing opinions regarding the properties they are evaluating and the homes they are evaluating them against. While one agent may think a home's condition is excellent, thus increasing its value, another agent may feel the same house is merely in good condition and will not add much extra value to it. It boils down to my original theory that determining a home's value or what it will sell for is not an exact science because it can be subject to many differing opinions.

Early on in my real estate career, I worked with certain financial institutions for the purpose of conducting

Brokers' Price Opinions or BPO's. These institutions wanted to get an idea of what a home was currently worth, most commonly due to the owners falling behind on their mortgage payments. The companies did not want a full-blown appraisal because the homes were still occupied and they were looking to do this behind the scenes, without the current owner's knowledge.

So, for a fee, I would drive by the property, take exterior photos, do some research in the MLS and fill out a two or three-page report supplied by the institution, providing them with an estimated opinion value. I did hundreds of these because it was an easy way to add steady, supplemental income to my uncertain real estate commissions. Unfortunately, appraisal organizations were up in arms over these evaluations, because they felt real estate agents were not supposed to be determining value. As a result, agents in my area were prohibited from conducting these reports, or else they could be reprimanded and subjected to fines.

By now you are starting to see a bit of the politics involved behind the scenes in the real estate business. You are also starting to understand how real estate agents and appraisers are not exactly the best of friends. Agents and appraisers have somewhat of a push-and-pull relationship due to their differing roles and methods of value.

My personal theory is that a home should be worth what a buyer is willing to pay for it in a free market economy. For example, if Bob Carpenter is willing to purchase my home for $350,000, shouldn't that be what it is worth? In actuality, yes, as long as there is no bank or lending institution involved. Lending institutions only want to lend the amount of money that the average buyer would pay should the lender have to foreclose on the home and try and get their money back. As long as the home is being financed, the amount a buyer is willing to pay has nothing to do with the way value is determined by today's standards.

You may be thinking, *"Okay Dave, that's great, but how do we determine the value of my home?"* Well, I am getting to that. I just wanted to give you some background to let you know the differing points of view regarding real estate valuations, and that it is not as simple as many people think.

My advice for determining your home's value is as follows: If your home is a cookie-cutter type property and there are dozens, if not hundreds, of them within a one-mile radius, then you should either contact a real estate agent and have him or her do a market analysis on your home or conduct one yourself using available online sales comparables from some of the websites I mentioned in Chapter 11.

Residential appraisers will be using the comparison approach and will be looking at many of those same sold comps. There is no sense in spending lots of money on a fee appraisal when finding alike homes of comparable value should not be that difficult. Remember, you are looking for the same sized homes of similar quality, upgrades, condition and in the same neighborhood and zip code as your property.

If, on the other hand, you live in a unique property or a contemporary type design that is much less common in your area, then it makes good sense to have a fee appraisal done to see what value a licensed appraiser will give it. You can reach out to a real estate agent either before or after this has been completed. Don't be surprised if the numbers are not what you expected, as they can seemingly come out of left field. Just make sure you have the appraiser explain how to read the report and break down its meaning in comparison to the other homes. Ask why the appraiser subtracted value for certain characteristics and added value for others. Also, ask how many appraisals they have done on homes such as yours.

The value the appraiser puts on your home can determine your next course of action. If you are satisfied and think the appraisal is fair and reflects the value you expected, then it's time to discuss listing your home. If you are upset and feel the numbers do not represent the value of your property then it's time to seek another opinion with either an agent or another licensed appraiser without discussing your prior appraisal amount. That will get you an additional unbiased opinion. Once completed, things should be starting to point in one direction or the other, hopefully for the better.

TIP: *When pricing your home, it's important that you are aware of the expenses you will incur with the sale. If you are selling by owner, your fees will typically include transfer taxes, the payoff of existing loans, unpaid utilities, along with any outstanding property taxes. If you are using a real estate professional to sell your home, you need to factor in the total commission amount when calculating your bottom line.*

Overpricing

Keep in mind that all of this is subjective to differing opinions. I once saw a real estate slide show that displayed three different pictures of the same property with a caption under each. The first slide showed a beautiful castle of a home and the caption underneath said, *This is how the owner sees their home.* The next picture showed a decent looking house with the caption underneath saying, *This is how a buyer sees your home.* The third picture showed a run-down shack and the caption stated, *This is how the appraiser sees your home.* While this example is extreme by all measures, there is an element of truth to it, especially since sellers can sometimes be too biased towards their property and may see it through rose-colored glasses. Much of this may be due to sentimental value, which has zero actual value in real estate appraisals.

Once you've done your homework and have been presented with at least one market analysis and perhaps one appraisal, it should be very clear where you are situated in the market place. If there are lots of similar homes for sale and the market is slow, you may want to price yourself a tad below market value, hoping to get a quick offer and perhaps spur on a bidding war due to its attractive price. One thing you don't want to do when pricing your home for maximum value is to overprice it and end up chasing the market with price reductions. If you price your home correctly, it will usually sell in a reasonable amount of time for the highest and best amount. If you price it too high, many buyers will believe that is what you expect to get and they will tend to move on.

In short, pricing your home for maximum value does not mean overpricing it. I have seen sellers overvalue their home only to watch them chase the market with price reductions, hoping for an offer. Had it been priced correctly from the beginning it would have sold sooner and thus achieved its highest amount.

For example, I once listed a really nice condominium located in a picturesque residential setting. I conducted a market analysis for the seller, and he agreed to list it on the high end of the scale. Happily, we received an offer the first week on the market. I felt that it was a very good contract since the buyer wrote attractive terms and it was only shy of full price by around $1,500. I informed my client that the first offer is typically the best (this is true) and that he should seriously consider accepting this offer, or at the very least, provide an attractive counteroffer. Since we had just listed the home one week ago, the seller felt empowered that he had a golden goose on his hands and countered their offer with his original asking price. I warned him that this was not a good counter-offer and that he should concede something. He disagreed and I informed the buyer's agent that the sellers were sticking to the original list price.

One day later, the buyer's agent informed me that the buyers were withdrawing their offer. Apparently, they were offended by the seller's unwillingness to concede and they would not pay full price for the home. Four months later, the house was still on the market at a 20K price reduction. We ended up selling it a couple of months later due to yet another price reduction.

The moral of the story is this—don't get too high and mighty about your home when you receive your first offer. Remember the story of the three homes I described above. Your home probably isn't the castle you may think it is. Take your first offer very seriously, because it will most likely be the best offer you get. When a house has not been on the market for long, buyers may be worried that they are competing with other buyers, and so they try to make a competitive offer (closer to the asking price). If a house has been on the market for a while, this fear is diminished, and the buyers feel there is more room for negotiation.

Also, be willing to negotiate something to let the buyer feel as if they are winners in the negotiations, even though you gave up very little and saved a lot of time, which can be your worst enemy when selling a home for its maximum value. Remember, the longer the house sits on the market, the lower your offers will become.

TIP: *In a good seller's market, it's a good idea to price your home slightly above what you want to get for the property in order to give yourself some wiggle room for negotiations. For example, if it looks as if a good market price for your home is $300,000, you should consider pricing it around $305,000 to enable you to move down on the price some without hurting your bottom line. Buyers like to feel they have won by having the seller come down on their price. It can make for a win-win situation.*

Lastly, keep in mind that no matter what a buyer is willing to pay for your home, you probably won't get it if the appraisal comes in low. Thus, your house really needs to be sold twice-once to the buyer and then to the appraiser. Don't hang firm on a price that may not appraise for value and thus waste lots of precious time and energy.

Hopefully, this chapter has shed some light on determining a home's value. It is very complex and is definitely not an exact science by any means. Do your homework so you will be confident in whatever price you decide on.

In the next chapter, I discuss the different types of seller's disclosures that may be required in your state in order to sell your home. Disclosures are legally binding, so you will want to take your time and answer the questions as best as you can. Sharpen your pencil, grab an eraser and I'll see you on the next page!

Chapter 13

The Dreaded Disclosures

"Get your facts first,
then you can distort them as you please."
~ Mark Twain

Disclosure documents typically include a *Lead-Based Paint Disclosure, Radon Disclosure,* and a general home disclosure form, where owners are required to put in writing if they have any knowledge of various conditions, either past or present, in their property and if any of them have been treated. The disclosure document that pertains to the main portion of the home is much more in-depth and complicated. Sellers' comments after seeing it for the first time have been, "How am I supposed to know all of this? I didn't build the house, I only lived in it!"

Disclosures are typically required by the state in which the property resides. They include a list of questions pertaining to the home's condition and other factors about the property of which a buyer would not otherwise have knowledge of such as the age of the furnace and central air conditioning, the age of the roof, how many existing layers of shingles there are, if any areas of the property accumulate water and if there are cracks and bulges in the foundation, etc. Sellers are faced with a choice of whether or not they are going to fix any of the defective conditions or simply disclose them.

If you are feeling overwhelmed, you are not alone. Just do the best you can and be as upfront and honest as possible. You may want to dig out the disclosures you received when you purchased the property to help refresh your memory. This will serve as a template regarding prior conditions and the type of systems your home has. Use a pencil to fill out the documents so you can easily make changes. Once you're finished, you can copy the forms on a copier for non-erasable duplicates. It's always a good idea to read the entire questionnaire before filling anything out because you will see other areas that are similar and you can avoid duplication of answers by just saying, *See answer to Question 10*, etc. If you are unsure whether you should mention something, ask yourself if you would want to know about it if you were the buyer.

TIP: *Many areas are cracking down on houses without home improvement permits. Examples of this are finished basements, outdoor decks, and porches, etc. Sometimes a seller can disclose the lack of permits and not be responsible for obtaining them. Be sure to check with your local real estate professionals to better determine how you should proceed.*

Chances are there are areas of your house which are less than perfect. For example, if you were to get seven inches of rain in a day, would your basement leak? Or is there a room in your home that lacks a central heating-ventilation-air-conditioning (HVAC) supply duct or return? Do you have some windows that don't want to stay open or that you can't open at all? If you said *yes* to any of these or are thinking of other areas in your home that are not perfect, then this chapter is for you.

Legal

Andrew P. Taylor, an attorney with Copeland Taylor, LLC says, "It is the seller's best interest to make full disclosure of all defects," implying that not doing so can come back to haunt the sellers later. He states, "Sellers also need to be careful about the accuracy of the material they post on social media and the legal ramifications if they are less than truthful," implying that boasting untruths about their property on social media is not advisable.

In most areas, by disclosing a defective item, the purchaser is buying the home with the knowledge of a defect and accepting it as is. The one exception to this rule is if the seller downplays the defect in the disclosure and the condition is much worse than what was stated.

For example, Mary Smith is selling a home that has several outlets that are not working. She lists these outlets in the seller's disclosure and puts the property up for sale. Tommy Jones makes a successful bid on Mary's house with the knowledge of the defective outlets. Tommy has a thorough home inspection where it is determined that the non-working outlets are the result of a defective electrical panel box, along with defective circuit breakers. Tommy's agent writes an endorsement to the agreement of sale requesting that Mary replace the electrical panel box and circuit breakers prior to settlement. Mary is furious and tells her agent she is not going to spend all that money when she disclosed up front that the outlets were not working. So, who is right?

This is a classic example of an all too common scenario that occurs after a home inspection. Negotiations over the home inspection report are the number one reason why sales agreements fall apart. Sellers feel they did their best at disclosing items and buyers say they never would have spent that much money to purchase the home had they known about all of the recently discovered home inspection defects.

In the above situation, Tommy has a better argument because even though Mary disclosed the non-working outlets, she did not disclose the defective panel box and circuit breakers. She simply did not know they were defective and feels disclosing the defective outlets also covered whatever reason there might be that they were not working. This is generally not considered to be the case, however. The new information turned up by the home inspection revealed the underlying cause, which was not covered in the seller's disclosure. Mary's lack of knowledge about the cause of the problem does not absolve her from having to make the necessary repairs or to compensate the buyers for this undisclosed flaw.

Because of the complexities of home inspection reports, it is much better to have two opposing real estate agents handle these problems, rather than the buyer and seller. Real estate agents also get heated at one another and argue these types of situations daily, but it won't "strain the marriage" to the point of divorce, as it may do if the buyer and seller were having to hash out this type of problem without assistance. Once that first stone is cast, the deal is doomed to fail. I've seen it happen when buyers and sellers start communicating directly with each other, thinking they are making the transaction easier for themselves, only to create a train wreck in the process.

In a second example, Bobby Brady writes an acceptable offer on 987 King St. He is thrilled about moving into his first home. Bobby has a home inspection that states *the roof is worn and nearing the end of its useful life and should be budgeted for replacement.*

Bobby, who is not using a real estate agent, tells the seller that he wants a new roof due to the home inspection report. Karen King, the seller, reminds him that she disclosed the roof was 29 years old and points out that the inspector did not indicate the roof was leaking, and thus it is doing what it is intended to do, which is to keep water out. Bobby is furious. He had no idea he was going to have to budget for a $10,000 roof replacement. The two have an argument and Bobby demands a new roof or the deal is off. Karen says farewell and the deal falls apart.

Who is right in this situation? Karen disclosed the age of the roof in the disclosure, not to mention that the roof is not actively leaking. But Bobby didn't know about its worn condition and diminishing life span. In short, age is not a defect. Technically, Karen did all the right things in disclosing everything she knew about the roof. Bobby should have done his homework on the average lifespan of a roof when he was preparing to purchase the property. It's not rocket science that a 29-year-old roof is close to needing replacement.

If the deal falls through, it hurts the seller because they have to put the house back on the market. Other interested parties will want to know why the deal fell apart. It will add an additional 45 to 60 days or more for the seller to market the property and close on the next deal. When a deal falls through for buyers, they will have spent hundreds of dollars on inspections and may stand to lose their interest rate lock. In short, a failed deal can be a lose-lose proposition for both parties.

In the above example, had the two not been dealing directly with each other, and instead used real estate agents to facilitate the transaction, it most likely would have resulted in a compromise. For example, the buyer and seller agree to split some of the cost of the roof and having the seller provide the buyer with a credit at closing.

These are two examples of a common home inspection train wreck that can easily derail a closing. Both parties need to keep an open mind and look at the big picture when these situations arise. Mary could have stood her ground; however, in the long run, it was better for her to give in a little and settle in order to get it over with. She could have opted to have a new roof installed and try to sell the house for a higher amount, but all of that takes time along with upfront costs, the hassle of dealing with contractors and the potential for delays and poor workmanship.

So, the question then becomes disclose, or fix and disclose? Much will depend upon the issue and how it will affect a buyer. For example, if the issue is water in the basement getting much of its contents wet, it's a no-brainer to fix it prior to listing the house. Sellers may balk at the idea of spending the money to repair the leak, but it will be cheaper in the long run if they do so. If they don't fix it, they are likely to get a reduced sales price along with a longer marketing period. Lastly, buyer uncertainty of the needed repairs to fix the water issues will often chase them away, since they are now forced into dealing with the problem themselves.

TIP: *Most areas require real estate agents to disclose any defects they know about a property. For example, if agent Bob Barker knows his listing at 354 Hollywood Drive has a roof leak, he is required to divulge this even though he is working for the seller. He has an obligation to disclose material defects since they are not considered confidential information. You need to be aware of this when speaking candidly with your agent.*

Please note that you will still need to disclose any prior defects along with any completed repairs to correct them. This is a perfect time to brag about the improvements you've made, such as, *Installed a new basement waterproofing system with battery back-up. No leaks since and the system has a 15-year transferable warranty to the new buyers.* This is the type of language a buyer will want to read.

Common Issues

Some common issues I see on a regular basis:

1. Broken seals in thermal, two-pane glass windows creating condensation between the glass.
2. Windows not staying in the up position, or which are difficult to open or close.
3. Curling roof shingles and/or algae on the roof.
4. Dirty HVAC systems.
5. Rooms with no air ducts or return vents.
6. Automatic garage doors not having electronic safety lasers, and/or doors that don't reverse when hitting stationary objects, along with older style door springs that lack a safety cable.
7. Mulch around the house is too high and touches the home's siding.
8. Landscaping is sloped towards the house, allowing water to accumulate against the foundation.
9. Clogged gutters with downspouts not directed away from the home's foundation.
10. Woodpile is stored next to the house (termite bait) and needs to be moved farther away.
11. Missing or loose handrails in stairwells.
12. Dishwasher discharge hose not high enough to prevent the backflow of water.
13. No ground fault circuit interrupter outlets (GFCI) and/or defective GFCI outlets in kitchens and baths, garage and basement.
14. Bathroom vent fans venting into the attic and need to be directed outdoors to prevent mold growth.
15. Dryer hose is improper material (fire hazard) and has too far of a run distance.

Make sure you check all of these areas before you list the home, or prior to a home inspection. One of the advantages of repairing ahead of time is you have all the work done before putting it under the microscope by the buyer's inspectors. Had you not corrected the issues ahead of time, the buyers may want to bring in their contractors to review it, which can open up another can of worms.

For example, Brian Wilson is selling his home and is aware of one window that is hard to open and close, so he discloses this. Grace Slick, the buyer, decides to have her window guy take a look. His subsequent report states, *Eventually all the windows will end up like the defective window and they should all be replaced.* Grace asks for all the windows to be replaced with the exception of the one window that was disclosed. Brian is furious. Had he just repaired the one window before listing his home, this situation would probably never have occurred. Now the entire deal is in jeopardy because Grace wants all new windows.

This is an extreme example, but things like this do happen, so it's best to be proactive when listing your home. Let's face it, contractors get paid for doing work. The more work they do, the more money they get paid. So, there is added incentive for them to suggest that more work needs to be done, rather than less. Also, keep in mind that contractors may increase the size of the job to make it something that would be worth their while to do.

Using your own contractors beforehand can save you money as opposed to having to do the repairs while under contract, where all eyes and expert opinions, such as the buyer's Uncle Fred and cousin Billy Bob, will want to stick their noses into the situation, making this deal more destined to fail. If you want to maximize your value, have home repairs completed prior to listing your home. No matter what you decide to do, be sure to fill out the disclosures as best as you can. Be observant and walk through your home while filling them out.

In the next chapter, I will review important security issues that you need to be aware of when selling your property. I will also review how to protect your personal possessions.

Chapter 14

Home and Personal Security

"Through the darkness which shrouds our prospects, the ark of safety is visible."
~Samuel Adams

Whether or not you decide to hire a professional real estate agent, there are always going to be security concerns. There are several issues you should address before buyers come marching through your home. Some of these may or may not apply to you when selling.
The issues are:

> ➢ Key Security
> ➢ Valuables
> ➢ Prescription Medicine
> ➢ Guns and Ammunition
> ➢ Hazards
> ➢ In-Home Cameras

Key Security

If you are selling the home by owner this topic does not apply to you, since you will be touring the buyers yourself. If, on the other hand, you will be hiring an agent to sell your home, this is important information that you should know.

The lockbox is a device that securely holds the key so real estate agents can easily access the property. For convenience, most lockboxes are attached to the home's front doorknob. There are primarily two different types of lockboxes that brokers and their agents use. One is a manual combination lockbox, the other is an electronic lockbox. Both of these enable the seller to exit the property during showings since it is best that they not be present.

The manual box is an older style that uses either a combination or a key to open the box. Combination boxes are much more common of the two. The good news is that all agents can show the home when given the combination. The bad news is that no one knows who has the combination. For example, if real estate agent Mary Luck accesses the combination box while her buyers are standing right behind her, how is Mary to know that her buyers didn't just see the combination, which could be used at a later date when Mary is not present? Response: She doesn't! This is one reason why I am not a fan of manual lockboxes. There is no way of knowing who has the combination to the box and can gain entry into the house anytime they want.

Conversely, electronic lockboxes are designed to work with electronic codes provided wirelessly. Only agents and affiliate members, such as home inspectors, have access to electronic lockboxes through their local Board of

Realtors®. If an agent is fired or loses their real estate license, they will not be able to obtain future access codes and thus will be unable to open any more electronic lockboxes. For even more accountability, electronic lockboxes document every time the box is accessed (time and date), along with the name of the person who opened it. This is invaluable information should something negative on the property occur. As a seller, you need to discuss your lockbox choices and choose what's best for your given situation.

Be sure not to have spare keys lying around the home or sticking out of the inside of door locks where someone can easily grab them. Don't leave anything to chance by securing all of your keys.

TIP: *Many electronic lockboxes can be programmed to operate at specific times of the day. For example, if you only want showings after 10:00 am and no later than 7:00 pm, many agents can program the box so that it will only dispense the key with these time parameters. Doing so will ensure that your lockbox will not be opened early in the morning, or late at night.*

Valuables

Since lots of people are going to be walking through your home, it's a great idea to secure your valuables ahead of time. Jewelry, spare cash, watches, stamp/coin collections, etc., should all be locked away somewhere safe. I personally have never had an issue with this, probably because I warn my clients in advance to be proactive. Theft is not commonplace within our industry, but you don't want to tempt fate. Just because a real estate agent will be accompanying buyers during showings, doesn't mean they can monitor all of the people that are present. A FSBO can't monitor everyone either. I have done tours where there are three generations of family members all looking at the home at the same time. One person can't accurately keep track of all of those people wandering about.

I am particularly concerned about children running around and inadvertently picking something up and sticking it in their pockets. Like the poker adage says, "We all trust one another, but let's cut the cards anyway." Best to put the valuables where they are safe and not leave anything to chance.

You will also want to lock up any important documents such as tax returns, bank statements, etc. No reason to leave these lying around exposing personal information such as your social security number. Your property will look much neater while giving you the peace of mind that your personal information remains private.

Prescription Medicine

It is important that you secure your meds, especially the opioid types and other ones sought by drug users. Again, it's not a fun topic, but it is worthy of review. You don't want anyone taking your medications with them, so you need to secure them by locking them up, or hiding them somewhere safe because your medicine cabinet is the first place they will look.

Pharmacies don't let strangers walk behind the pharmacy counter and you shouldn't give buyers access to your meds either. Besides, it's a privacy issue that no one should be aware of except you and your doctor.

Guns and Ammunition

I am always amazed at how many times I will see someone's unlocked guns hanging on a wall or behind an unlocked glass cabinet. It doesn't take much imagination to realize that this is not good practice. At the very least, you should have locked trigger guards on them, so that the triggers cannot be pulled. It is best that you have them locked away and out of sight of visitors. Today's open house guest could be tomorrow's burglar, so don't give them the opportunity.

Lastly, ammunition should also be discretely put away. You don't want someone grabbing bullets out of your ammo box during a tour. If they are used in a crime, it could pull you into it, so please make sure you secure your guns and ammo.

__NOTE__: While editing this book, I toured buyers through a $450K contemporary home in a very nice residential area. While viewing the property, the buyer informed me that the master bathroom did not have enough storage for her things. In reviewing the situation, I opened one of the vanity drawers to better determine its storage capacity and noticed a very large, loaded handgun with a cocked hammer sitting inside. This had a very negative impact on me and the buyer. A short time after leaving, I received a message from her that they were no longer interested in the home. I am convinced *the loaded gun played a large part in that decision. Be smart about storing your weapons because they may turn off a potential buyer from pursuing your property.*

Hazards

It's a good idea to take a walk through your property looking for hazards that could hurt unsuspecting visitors. Broken or missing steps, loose handrails, uneven flooring, exposed wiring, mouse traps, rodent poison, doors opening to a stairless 10-foot drop, and an uncovered backyard well are all things I have witnessed while touring properties.

Imagine that a young family is looking at your home and their three-year-old breaks free from her mother's grasp and discovers and sets off a mousetrap on the pantry floor. This is not going to bode well for you, or anyone for that matter, so please do your best to carefully assess your home for potential hazards an unsuspecting buyer may encounter.

It is easy to forget about issues that may have existed for weeks, months or even years. You need to make a conscious effort to minimize the dangers that are in your house, or at the very least, give appropriate notification so that agents and their clients will be better prepared for what lies ahead. A sign on the door such as "Do Not Open-Stairs Not Built Yet" will let visitors know of a potentially dangerous situation.

In-Home Cameras

Home surveillance is all the rage these days, especially doorbell cams. Cameras are a great way to keep you informed about what's going on inside and outside your home. However, there are some important considerations to keep in mind.

Some states are now requiring the seller to disclose, in writing, if they have any active electronic surveillance equipment, either audio, video or both. I have witnessed buyers become uptight after realizing they are being recorded while touring properties with active surveillance equipment. The buyers act as if the seller is actually in the home while they look around. In the previous chapter, we discussed how it would be best if you vacate your home during showings. By video recording your guests, they may be feeling intimidated and less able to relax and enjoy viewing your home.

When salespeople or sellers hover around a buyer whether it be in a department store or a pre-owned home, buyers get apprehensive and have difficulty relaxing. The same thing can occur when buyers feel they are under constant surveillance, which can make them apprehensive and less likely to feel good about their overall experience. When buyers don't have a warm and fuzzy feeling while visiting your home, they are less likely to buy. They may not even be able to put their finger on why they don't wish to pursue your home for purchase. They just know, "it's not the right house for them."

While it is interesting to observe all of this on your monitoring equipment, it is less than thrilling for your buyers to feel "watched" while they are walking around your home. It's important to remember the reason why there are strangers inside your home in the first place. Because you want to sell your home and they happen to be in the market for a new home. These visitors should be seen as guests and less like criminals. It is for this reason that you should consider shutting off interior monitoring during daytime tours and resuming them once they have concluded. You would want this detail expressed in the seller's disclosure so the buyers will know the status of the cameras.

Personally, I don't want to give buyers any reason to be negative while touring a property of mine. The more relaxed I can make them feel, the better. I always make sure the heat and air conditioner are set at a comfortable temperature even if the home is vacant. Yes, this costs extra to do so, but the more comfortable they are while touring, the longer they will stay. The longer they stay, the better chance they will "feel at home" and want to write an offer to purchase.

Andrew P. Taylor, an attorney with Copeland Taylor, LLC says he foresees legal issues with sellers not disclosing that they have video cameras recording while the buyers are touring their property. He says, "Sellers should give notice throughout the house that the buyers are being recorded, and not doing so could violate the purchaser's privacy rights."

Happy, content and comfortable buyers purchase homes. Wary, uncomfortable and intimidated buyers scurry out the door to tour the next property. Make a conscious decision about how you want to handle your electronic devices.

Recently, I worked with home sellers who totally understood this and decided to remove the interior camera and only monitor the exterior of the home during showings. This way they could see anyone that came and went, but were not actively watching and listening to the buyer's tour.

TIP: *Once your house is officially on the market, you may notice cars slowly driving past your home at all hours of the day. Since the cat is now "out of the bag," lots of people may take an interest in your property with or without an appointment. This can include people walking around the perimeter of your house unannounced. Take noted precautions by locking all windows and doors. Be careful about opening your home to strangers without scheduled appointments. A visible front yard For Sale sign with contact info is all they need to get additional information.*

It's important that you take the necessary steps to ensure that your home is safe, secure and ready for visitors. Don't give them the opportunity to examine your costly and most sensitive things. Be prudent and remove them from the home, or lock them up. Make sure you have a plan when dealing with any surveillance equipment that you own and do what you think is best for your family and current home sale.

In the next chapter, I will review some last-minute preparations in order to get your home on the market. You are almost there, so turn the page and let's get to it.

PART V:

MARKETING & INCENTIVES

Chapter 15

Marketing Your Home

"Creativity is intelligence having fun."
~Albert Einstein

It is now time to expose your beautiful property to the rest of the world, especially those seeking a home in your area. If you are using a real estate agent, much of this will be taken care of automatically. If you are marketing the property yourself, we will review the various steps in detail.

The strategies we will be reviewing are:

- Signs
- Print Advertising
- Internet
- Dedicated Website
- Social Media
- Multiple Listing Service
- Friends, Family, and Co-Workers

Signs

The first and most elementary way to market your home is to have a bright, visible sign in the front yard. Signs should basically notify passersby that the house is for sale and who they should contact for additional information. I have had several sellers tell me, "I don't want a sign in the yard because I don't want my neighbors to find out I'm moving." My typical response has been, "Don't you think they'll notice the attached lockbox, cars parked in the driveway and strangers going in and out of your house all day long?" Some sellers will give in and see how silly it appears. Others will be adamant about not wanting a sign.

Statistically, real estate signs account for approximately 6% of real estate sales, which is a good indication that they provide definite value. While installing listing signs, I have been approached by numerous people asking me all sorts of questions about the homes I am listing. There are still a good number of buyers on the market who will hop into the car and drive to their favorite areas of town in search of *For Sale* signs. I know, because I have received many calls off of signage and have sold homes this way. To exclude your property from having a sign is to eliminate many of these buyers, especially if they are not Internet savvy. Since it can help sell your home and your neighbors are going to find out anyway, you may as well add them to your marketing toolbox.

TIP: *Signs can be confiscated by your local officials for a variety of reasons, including putting them too close to busy roadways. Most FSBO signs are not as scrutinized as broker* *signs and not as likely to incur fines. If you are selling the home yourself, be sure to check and see what are the guidelines are in your area. Typically, a front-yard sign should be perfectly fine depending upon where it's placed.*

Print Advertising

I have found postcards to be an effective way to market homes. *Just Listed* postcards get the phones ringing and can stir up interest in your property. Fliers are also a handy way to display your home on bulletin boards throughout the community. Make sure you include some of your best professional photos.

Newspapers and print advertising are considered somewhat as dinosaurs these days due to the Internet and its broad reach. Although some agents still utilize newsprint, there are better choices that are far less expensive. In my area, print advertising is mainly used to promote weekend open houses. Unless you live in a place where the local newspaper is one of the main sources of information, I think you can forgo this medium

Internet

The Internet is doing to print media what the automobile did to the horse and buggy. Real estate information is now readily available all over the Internet and it has forever changed how many of us get our information.

When the Internet first became popular, some speculated that it would be the end of real estate agents and their brokers. However, due to the complexity of real estate transactions combined with the multitude of rules and regulations, this is still a long way off in the future. There are many different sites dedicated to real estate, such as *www.zillow.com*, *www.trulia.com*, *www.realtor.com*, etc. Be sure to revisit Chapter 11 for some additional sites.

There are many different ways to market a property on the Internet, the first of which is having your own website.

Dedicated Website

Many accomplished brokerages will provide you with your own website should you list your property with them. The site will contain professional photos, along with a complete property description to include room measurements, access to school data, systems information and other pertinent facts. It will also provide the viewer access to the listing agent for showings.

Websites are a great way to market your home because the site's address or URL can be advertised in print media and distributed in various other ways. For example, when your home is first put on the market, *Just Listed* postcards can be sent out with the included web link, thus providing easy access to loads of valuable information and photos. It's important to have your own dedicated web page when selling your home.

Social Media

Social media is doing to letters what DVDs did to VHS tapes many years ago. Now, most written correspondence is done via email, text and social media sites. Since most of your friends know you are in the process of selling your home, you should post information about your home sale on Facebook, LinkedIn, Twitter, Pinterest, Instagram and any other social media outlets you happen to frequent.

Be sure to include photos, along with a short blurb with the highlights of your property. You will also want to provide a link to the dedicated web page you set up that includes your contact information if you are selling the home yourself. If you are using an agent, be sure to include their contact information. It's probably best to leave the property disclosures off of the Internet and only provide them when purchasers visit your home or send them out upon request.

Multiple Listing Service - MLS

The multiple listing service is an Internet-based real estate information database brokers and agents use to list their properties. It is the best way to reach qualified buyers because it is the most accurate and up-to-date real estate data site. If you have hired an agent, you should automatically have your home listed in the MLS. This medium is accessible to those with a paid subscription and who are licensed agents, brokers or affiliates. Even though you need to be a subscriber of the MLS, data is permitted to be sent to buyers for their review.

There are ways sellers can get their property listed in the MLS without hiring a real estate agent. For example, *FlatFeeMLS.net* offers MLS access for a fee that is lower than that of typical brokerages. This will get your home into the MLS and viewed by its many agents and brokers. Keep in mind that due to the low entry fee, you will be offering a

very low compensation rate to agents who have the potential
to sell your home. Additional information on this topic is
included in Chapter 10, *The Truth about Commissions*. As
previously noted, this is not the best way to get agents to
show and sell your home, but sites such as this are good for
FSBO's wanting to go it alone yet still be listed in the MLS.

If you do decide to go this route, keep in mind that
you will be inundated with telephone calls from agents
wanting to list your home. All of your contact
information will be visible online, making you ripe for
solicitations.

TIP: *I have witnessed MLS listings being copied and pasted
into sites such as Craigslist with false information, such as
that the house is **For Rent** at below-average rental prices. It
will include photos, along with much of the same verbiage.
This is a scam intended to dupe renters into sending a
deposit check to the fraudsters for a nonexistent rental. You
may want to be proactive and check the site and/or
Google your address to see what information comes up.
Notify local authorities if your home has been targeted and
make sure everyone who contacts you about the home
understands it is **For Sale** and not for rent.*

Friends, Family, and Coworkers

Be sure to utilize as much marketing power as you can,
especially if you are selling the property yourself. Enlist your
friends, family and coworkers to help spread the word about
your great home. One way is to have cards printed out with a
picture of your property, its address and the website URL.

Hand these out to everyone you know and ask them to pass the cards along to anyone who is in the market to purchase a home.

You can even post them on bulletin boards at the library, coffee shop, grocery store, etc., and hand them out while on personal appointments to the beauty salon, auto repair shop, doctor's office or anywhere else. Some sellers are a little squeamish about doing this, which is why I provide these cards on an as-needed basis. The more buyers who know about your home, the better your chance of selling it.

Lastly, *Open Houses* deserve some mention as they can attract interested buyers who have not been working with an agent. Producing a sale from one is infrequent, but it does occasionally happen. Be sure to read Chapter 17 where I devote the entire chapter to this topic.

Marketing plays a key role in exposing your property to the public. There are many different ways this can be achieved by casting a wide net and utilizing all of the different tools, such as good signage, social media, a dedicated website, and the MLS, third party websites, along with friends, family, and coworkers. Be sure to take advantage of the many different forums to market your home.

In the next chapter, I will review the final preparations for showing your property. There are many things to think about before you open the door to potential suitors, so let's get started.

Chapter 16

The Show Must Go On

"Inside my heart is breaking,
my makeup may be flaking,
but my smile still stays on."
~Queen

      You have spent weeks getting your home ready for buyers, and it is now show-time! There are some important steps that you need to know in order to empower your home to have the best chance of selling for maximum profit. They are:

- Photographs
- Staging
- NAR Statistics
- Listing Materials
- Pets
- Lights Up – Thermostat On
- Showings
- Feedback

Photographs

It's now time to get some professional photos to display your home's sparkle and accentuate its wonderful features. For fixer-uppers, foreclosure homes and properties not in the best of condition, I take the pictures myself utilizing a good, high megapixel camera. However, for well-maintained properties, I recommend getting a trained photographer, since they have the best equipment and the most experience in taking impressive photos.

I like to provide my sellers with a professional real estate photographer who will properly light and photograph the home. When the property has a spectacular setting, they provide the ability to have aerial photographs made with a drone. I don't feel these are necessary with some conventional homes, but I will provide them if the seller insists. Lastly, I have seen computer satellite images also look satisfactory in presentations.

When completed, the photos can be uploaded into the MLS and used in various marketing materials. Be sure to have your home photo-ready before the photographer visits. This means no kitchen dryer racks on the counter, trash cans have been tucked away, along with anything else you do not want to have photographed. It's also a good idea to move cars out of the driveway and put them on the other side of the street. Professional photographers won't want to move your things for you, so be prepared when they arrive.

Try to schedule the appointment around noon on a predicted sunny day. This will provide good lighting and reduce shadows. The main purpose of the photographs is to make the house look its best and entice buyers to visit your home. The greater the number of buyer tours, the better the chance of getting an offer.

Staging

If your property is vacant or is filled with obsolete furniture, you should consider staging your home. This is done by moving in new furniture, window coverings, plants, knickknacks, tables and chairs to help bring your home into the 21st Century. When a property is in showroom condition with beautiful furnishings, buyers will want to stay longer as they envision themselves living and entertaining friends and family in such a well-appointed house.

Mary Karakashian, a member of the Association of Property Scene Designers (APSD) and owner of Unique Home Staging and Design, LLC says, "The more time you give yourself to prepare and plan for staging your home, the less stressful the process will be. Staging is a great service that can help you sell your home faster and possibly for more money!"

Most brand-new model homes are professionally staged by interior designers who meticulously furnish the property with exquisite plants, ornaments, window coverings, along with a beautiful family room, dining room, and bedrooms. Homebuilders know a gorgeous model home is the best way to sell vacant homes since buyers can visualize how wonderful their place can be. I have toured many newly-constructed model homes and have been blown away by the meticulous touches and color schemes that accentuate the houses they are displaying. Even though I was bringing buyers through and not wanting to purchase a property myself, I wanted to stay, relax, watch television and have a snack, which is exactly what was intended. Potential buyers who feel at home in a property are more likely to make it their home.

NAR Statistics

The National Association of REALTORS® (NAR) has compiled statistics on home staging and notes the following with regards to pricing, marketing time and overall impact on buyers:[2]

Sellers' agents survey of staged properties percentage change in dollar value:
- 46% of sellers' agents reported an increase in the price of staged homes in comparison to similar homes
- 19% of sellers' agents felt that staging had no impact on the sales price and
- 33% of sellers' agents were unsure

Sellers' Agents survey of staged properties and marketing time:
- 25% felt staging greatly decreased marketing time
- 28% felt staging slightly decreased marketing time
- 12% felt staging had no impact on marketing time

---

[2] National Association of REALTORS® Research Group - 2019 Profile of Home Staging. Reprinted with permission.

- 18% unsure if staging had an impact on marketing time
- 18% felt staging increased marketing time

Impact on Buyers Viewing a Staged Home

- 83% found it easier to visualize as a future home
- 38% more willing to tour after seeing it online
- 37% feel it will positively impact value if decorated to buyer's tastes
- 23% are more willing to overlook other property faults
- 7% felt it will negatively impact value if decorated against buyer's taste

I have witnessed sellers not wanting to spend the money on staging, only to end up with numerous price reductions far exceeding the potential cost of staging. Thus, staging can be more cost-effective in the long run by achieving a quicker sale along with a higher selling price that exceeds the staging costs.

Most staging companies give free estimates and they will at the very least provide you with some good ideas. If your home furnishings are dated or the home is vacant, it is well worth the effort to consider having your home staged.

Listing Materials

There are certain materials you should distribute to buyers so they can review important aspects of your home and recall many of its fine features. Some buyers will only take this information if they are interested in the property, while others will take anything free that you have to offer.

I recommend providing a property description sheet which details room dimensions and other important facts about the house, along with pertinent area and school information. You can also include information about the homeowner association and any activities they organize, such as holiday gatherings, community days, etc.

It's also appropriate to have the property disclosures available so the buyer can review them while they are at the home. Proficient listing agents will bundle all of the information into a colorful brochure with a welcome note. It's important to include plenty of professional photos to help prospective buyers recall your house in the coming days. When buyers visit six-to-eight houses within a short period of time, they tend to forget important details, such as which home had the wonderful stone fireplace and which had the master bedroom suite with Jacuzzi tub, etc. A colorful brochure is a good reminder of the home's highlights and features.

Pets

People love their pets, but they won't necessarily love your pets. This can be especially true with homebuyers who don't have any pets at all. People without them are typically very sensitive to pet odors, so you want to ensure this is not the first thing that greets them at the door. Best to have your furry friends as clean and fresh smelling as possible, along with their bedding and toys.

I will never forget the time I was touring a home with buyers in a dimly lit property. The home was occupied and there were contents strewn all around the home. I was leading my clients into a dark basement when all of a sudden, "BARK, BARK, BARK, GROWL, BARK, BARK, BARK, GROWL!!!!" I must have jumped two feet off the ground. Thankfully, the dog was in a cage and unable to attack us, but the absolute terror of this event was jarring and detrimental to our visit, since everyone was now in a state of shock and just wanted to leave the home. I didn't know dogs were capable of lying in wait for strangers and always assumed they barked upon entry to scare off visitors. Live and learn.

The lesson is this: Sellers should provide buyers with ample warning if there are any pets that will remain in the house during showings. Some buyers are terrified of dogs and cats and deserve the courtesy of being warned ahead of time. This is also significant, because your visitors may have pet allergies.

It's also important to post whether or not the pets are allowed outside. I once accidently let an indoor cat into the backyard during a tour and it took me approximately 15 minutes to catch it. I've also witnessed cats wanting to enter a home that I am touring and have no idea if it actually lives there, or is just trying to get warm or ransack the place.

TIP: *If you don't want the world to know about your pets, make sure you notify the appointment center about them, so only actual buyers touring the home will be alerted. It's also a good idea to leave some signage inside the home reminding everyone about your animals, along with any important instructions, such as:* **Do not stick fingers into the cage. Brutus may bite.**

I have also seen sellers let their "friendly" dogs run freely during tours only to have them behave a little too friendly by sniffing everyone's crotch and hanging all over the guests. Although the pet is your best friend, buyers may prefer not to be "hounded" when visiting your home. It's best to leave your furry companions with friends and family or put them into a temporary cage while buyers are perusing your property. Remember, this is only temporary. The longer a buyer stays in your house, the better the chance they will be writing an offer.

Not everyone has the same affection for pets as their owners, so be respectful of your visiting guests. Lastly, make sure you remove any pet piles in the yard. Buyers will not take kindly to stepping in them while on your property, not to mention they may track it back inside your home. You will also want to empty your cat's litter box on a regular basis to keep the home smelling fresh.

Lights Up – Thermostat On

Ever notice when you walk into a retail store that all the lights are on and the temperature is at a comfortable setting? Do you think this is a coincidence? It is no accident that retailers keep their rooms bright and comfortable to attract and retain buyers as long as possible. Some shops will even play soft, pleasant music and fill the air with delightful aromas to entice shoppers to stay longer. The reason is simple. The more comfortable and content a shopper is, the better chance they will stick around and purchase more goods.

You should adopt the same mindset. Turn on all of the lights and set the temperature to a comfortable level. Use floor lamps to brighten rooms that lack overhead lights. Open window shades and blinds to let in even more sunlight.

I have heard sellers say, "I don't want to spend money on keeping the house bright and running the heat and/or air conditioner while I'm not there." Trust me, you will be spending more money on price reductions than you will on added energy costs if you don't leave the home well-lit and comfortable. You can always set timers or turn the lights off and readjust the thermostat after the showings.

Even if the house is vacant, it's important that the temperature is at a comfortable level. I have witnessed buyers walk into freezing cold homes and walk out within minutes because they couldn't take the cold, and I was right behind them! If buyers are uncomfortable, they will be thinking more about vacating your property and less about buying it.

Showings

You need to decide if you want buyers and their agents to remove their shoes when touring your property. If your home is a cream puff, I recommend that you have signage at the front door which states: *Please remove your shoes or wear the provided booties when touring this fine home.* Your agent can provide you with the signage and booties and also notify the appointment center to inform the buyers in advance that they will be requested to remove their shoes. Don't take these extra precautions if your floors are not worthy of it. I have witnessed buyers become put-off at having to wear booties in homes with dirty floors and carpets. Be sure to provide interior and exterior doormats to limit the amount of debris that is tracked into the home. Without doormats, buyers will have no place to wipe their shoes before entering your home.

You have now managed to pick up the house and put everything away. The lights are turned on and the home is a comfy 70 degrees. The brochures are neatly placed on a table near the front door and the pets are at Uncle Doug's house. The home smells of pastries and fresh coffee from this morning's feast. Everything is set for your first appointment of the day. It's now time to gather a few of your things and head out the door for some personal time so you can give the buyers and their agent some space to preview your immaculate property.

Some sellers like to bake bread or cookies before showings to make buyers feel at home. I think this is a fabulous idea, along with putting some samples out for your guests along with some bottled water and a "help yourself" sign. Be careful not to bake something too gooey, or else you may find yourself with a mess later on. I learned this the hard way when conducting open houses with food.

It's also a good idea to arrange some fresh flowers to put in the kitchen and dining room. There is something about beautiful fresh flowers that stimulate people to feel their best.

If you are not sure what to do with yourself, I'll give you some suggestions my clients have followed. How long has it been since you visited your public library? If it's been a while, you will be amazed at all of the materials they have. I like stopping in and perusing the out of state newspapers and various magazines to which I don't subscribe. I've also had clients go to the movies when they have lots of showings in one day. It's a great way to kill some time and stay abreast of the new releases. Other clients have visited the local zoo during heavy touring hours.

One thing you shouldn't do is hang around the house, on the porch or even directly outside. Buyers are leery when they see sellers hovering around and possibly listening in on their conversations. Even if you are not, they will think you are, and it will make them uncomfortable. Best to get in the car and leave. Since you've made an effort to put away all your valuables, medications and important documents, your home should be fine. The sooner you procure a buyer, the sooner you can halt showings and stop the madness. Make the showings really count by giving the buyers lots of time and space.

Feedback

You will want to have a plan for receiving comments from parties who have toured your home. Getting valuable feedback from buyers and agents is a wonderful way to determine if changes are in order. If you start to see more than one of the same issues, such as "pet odor," it's time to think seriously about having the carpets shampooed or replaced. Perhaps it is something else, but whatever it is, you should address the problem so it does not stay an issue. Once corrected, you can have your agent notify all of the buyer's agents who previously visited the home about the new carpet and that the house is now free of odors. This way they will know to revisit the property for another tour.

Most agent feedback is now done via email with questionnaires being sent from the listing agent to the buyer's agent. For example, John Denver is the listing agent for 123 Main Street. The home had two showings today and he has sent both buyer's agents an email requesting they fill out the brief feedback form. Once the forms are completed, they will automatically be sent to John's email, where he can review them and contact the seller to share the data. Most questions are as follows: *Is your buyer interested in pursuing this home? What was your overall impression of the home? Was it priced appropriately? What suggestions do you have for improving the salability of the property? Will your buyer be writing an offer? Why or why not?*

These questions are designed to smoke out any underlying reasons why a buyer will or will not be pursuing the purchase of your home.

If buyer's agents do not fill out the form in a timely fashion, I will follow up with a polite phone call asking for their feedback. This will usually nudge them to complete the form. Some feedback may sound ridiculous, such as "House only has a one car-garage," which is the same number of garages that are listed in the MLS and is visible from the street. I've heard the same general comments with bedrooms and baths, which were also disclosed in advance of their showing. Apparently, some buyers don't do much research when touring properties.

Other times the feedback will be spot on, such as *Buyers did not care for the pink walls.* It is probably a good idea to neutralize the pink into an off-white color. Constructive feedback will provide you with the information you need to increase your home's chance of selling for maximum value.

In the next chapter, I will be discussing the pros and cons of having an open house. Grab some tasty hors-d'oeuvres and meet me on the next page!

Chapter 17

Open Houses
Brokers Open

*"The greatest fear in the world
is of the opinions of others.
And the moment you are unafraid of the crowd you
are no longer a sheep, you become a lion."*
~Osho

One way to expose your property to the general
public is to have an open house. I have mixed feelings about
open houses because there is no way to qualify the buyers
beforehand to ensure they have the financial wherewithal to
purchase your home. Since there is no way of qualifying
them before their visit, you have no way of knowing what the
purpose of their visit is. Do they truly want a new house, or
are they touring it for decorating ideas or worse yet, for
unscrupulous reasons? Not to be negative, but I have seen
some interesting characters come through open houses and
would bet they were not looking to purchase the property.

TIP: *In a previous chapter I discussed securing your valuables before having buyer tours in your home. This is especially important if you plan on holding an open house. I have had twenty or more people come through a property at the same time and it's nearly impossible to keep track of everyone and everything. Make sure you secure all of your valuables, meds, etc., before conducting one.*

Unwanted Guests

When allowing total strangers inside your home without having them pre-qualified by a mortgage lender, you are opening the door to all different types of people who may not even be able to purchase your car, let alone your home. It is just not possible to keep tabs on everybody in the house, because they may be scattered about. When hosting a very busy open house, I try to stay near the front door to be able to monitor everyone who is leaving.

I remember I was holding an open house at a large two-story property when a disheveled couple walked in the door. They were not interested in signing into the logbook and didn't want to small talk about the home in the least. Once they blew past me, I noticed they quickly separated and went their different ways. This struck me as odd and my sixth sense kicked in, warning me that their visit was probably in search of prescription medicines or valuables that could be easily snatched. I immediately went outside and took a picture of their vehicle and license plate, just in case something was reported as stolen later.

It's doubtful the couple would have ever been able to tour the house in the first place if not for the open house.

Most agents will ensure that their prospects be prequalified by a mortgage lender before working with them. Without that knowledge, you have no way of knowing their ability to purchase your home. Some agents will try and pre-qualify prospects with questions before they tour properties with them such as: *Where do you live now? Are you renting or do you own? Have you been pre-qualified by a lender? If so, who is the company and loan officer? If not, why not? I can have a mortgage lender call you today. What's the best number for them to reach you?* Once these questions have been posed, it's pretty obvious who is a potential homebuyer and who is not. Since we all work on commissions, we need to be careful with whom we spend our time.

Other frequent visitors to open houses are nosy neighbors. They wait until the owners have left and then they head on over to "see what the Jones's are up to." Sometimes they will announce themselves as neighbors, while other times they won't, and I will be tipped off by someone else currently inside the home.

Problems

During another open house I conducted, a guest grabbed some tools out of the garage and was headed toward the front door for a quick getaway. I asked him what he was doing, and he said, "The owner had borrowed these months ago and I'm just taking them back." I informed him that he would need to bring this up with the seller and if he didn't return them to the garage, I would be forced to call the police. He could tell I was serious and returned them and left without another word. Had I not been standing near the front door those tools would have been long gone. I have no idea whether he was really a neighbor of the sellers or just an open house burglar wanting to expand his tool collection.

This is just another example of the type of guests you may get at your open house and why some agents are squeamish about holding them and others refuse to have them at all. There are far worse happenings that have occurred at open houses which thankfully have never happened to me.

When I host open houses, I try to be as chatty as I can by asking questions to better determine how serious they are about buying a home. This way, I learn who I should spend more time with and who is just browsing. One time I asked a couple of women about their interest and they candidly told me they visit open houses solely for decorating ideas. I thanked them for being up front and told them they were welcome to look around, and to please let their friends and family know about the fine home.

My point is this–activity does not always translate into productivity because the activity may not be that of actual buyers.

While working in real estate since 1998, I have only had three open houses where I wrote an offer on the house with the buyer that was accepted by the seller. It was a wonderful experience to behold, especially since I received the lion's share of the commissions. Unfortunately, this is the exception and not the rule, as few open houses result in a sale.

If you do want an open house, it's probably best to hold it the first week of showings, where you should get lots of actual buyers wanting to compete for your home. Or you may choose to hold it at a later date if the house does not sell right away. Some buyers will be turned off by the competition of the former while others will not. Do what you feel is best for your home.

Broker's Open House

A broker's open house is another way to expose the property to area real estate agents who may have potential buyers. In my experience, they have typically been held after the property has been on the market for a while. When agents want qualified, professional feedback on one of their listings, they will hold a broker's open house for area agents to visit.

For them to get good attendance, they will typically advertise lunch and feed everyone who shows up. Sometimes they will promote a gift card drawing of up to $100 to sweeten the pot and to get as many attendees as possible. Occasionally, a visiting agent will discover that the home is a good fit for their buyer, but oftentimes this is not the case, since the property has previously been exposed to the MLS and the buying public.

While attending a broker's open, it is customary for the listing agent to present a questionnaire to the visiting agents asking for written feedback about the property. The questions are similar to buyer questionnaires but are more specific, such as: *At what price do you think the house will sell? What are the positive and negative attributes of this house? What improvements should be done to the home and do you think they are necessary and cost effective? Do you have a buyer who would be interested in this property?*

In my opinion, gathering agents feedback is the best reason to have a broker's open house, so you can get a professional consensus as to why the house isn't selling, sort of a second opinion on the property.

I have witnessed brokers open houses appear more like real estate agent reunions, since they can attract representatives from all different companies. It is true, the more people exposed to your property, the better the chances you have of selling it. However, broker's open houses are not the best example of this. If they were, more agents would have them at the beginning of the listing process and not wait until the house was on the market for an extended amount of time.

If your agent offers to hold a broker's open house, don't be surprised afterward if you receive a price reduction request to help sell the home, since this is often what the feedback will dictate.

I am not a big fan of brokers open houses and rarely conduct them but will do so if my clients insist. Should I want other agent's opinions, I'll generally ask them individually to visit the property with me. I find this to be much easier and less disruptive to my sellers.

Open houses and broker's open houses are another way of gaining additional exposure for your property. Just beware of the pros and cons of each, so you can decide if you want to participate.

In the next chapter, I will explore why your home is not getting offers. It's important to discover what's going on and fix it as soon as you can to keep your days on market to a minimum. Grab your notebook and let's get going!

Chapter 18

Why is my Home
Not Selling?

*"Success is going from failure to failure without a loss
of Enthusiasm."*
~Winston Churchill

Occasionally, I will experience a charming house that
for all intents and purposes should have sold but hasn't.
There can be lots of different reasons why a house has not
sold, and we will review them in this chapter.

To begin with, let's start with the basics. How are
homes currently selling in the immediate area of the
property that are of similar size, amenities and price?
Sometimes the market will experience lulls where there are
just not many buyers needing to purchase a home. Sure,
there are lots of tire kickers who will attend the open houses,
but they may just be looking to see "what the Smiths are up
to," and not be serious buyers.

As we discussed previously, you must receive feedback from buyer's agents regarding the recent showings you've had. Are there any reoccurring negative sentiments that are holding buyers back? For example, if several feedback comments mention driveway settlement cracks, perhaps they are not pursuing the home because they are afraid of what the cracks represent down the road in the form of expensive repairs. Remember, the majority of buyers are looking for the least amount of work in their next home, so when they notice potential future repairs, they may decide to pass on your property. It might be as simple as painting some dark rooms to a neutral color. I have seen buyers be very narrowminded when it comes to simple fixes. Some purchasers will consider minor paint jobs to be *too much work.*

Odors

A common buyer turnoff is unpleasant odors in a home. If you have pets, they should be clean, along with the areas in the home in which they frequent. Buyers aren't going to discern if the odor will be going with the sellers or not. If they smell something they don't like, they won't be getting the warm fuzzies and will simply move on to the next property.

I know from my experience of living with pets, we rarely notice our pets' odors because we've become desensitized to it. Ask a neighbor or good friend for their honest opinion. If you do have unwanted aromas, you will want to clean your carpets and other areas with an enzymatic based cleaner that will neutralize any existing pet urine that may be the cause. You may also try an air purifier to enhance your home's air quality. Don't overdo it with plug in deodorizers, though, as they can be overwhelming and cause buyers to think you're trying to hide something major, like mold. I have heard this directly from buyers in properties we've toured with as many as three to six plug-in deodorizers. If they think you're hiding something, they will move on to the next property.

Selling a home with pets is a lot harder than selling a home without them. Be sure to pay added attention to their cleanliness, as it can affect your sale.

Lighting

If your home doesn't have a lot of natural light, such as skylights, you should consider leaving most lights on during showings. I know of some buyer's agents who are not very diligent about turning on the lights when touring homes. Lighting can have a dramatic effect on how the house is seen and perceived. Think about all the money movie studios put into lighting their movies scenes. Lighting is huge, so make sure your house is well lit. Add floor lamps to rooms with no overhead lighting. Purchase additional lamps if your home is vacant and lacking enough light.

Clutter

Have you decluttered your property so it exemplifies spaciousness, with plenty of room for buyers to comfortably navigate your home? For example, I had a listing appointment for a woman whose father had recently died, and she wanted to sell the property. Unfortunately, her father was a hoarder and I could barely walk through the family room because there was so much stuff in the way. I couldn't even see the windows to determine what kind of condition they were in. It was even hard to tell the size of the room because it had been swallowed up with junk.

I informed her the only way to get the maximum value for the house was to remove all of its contents. Otherwise it would sell at a bare bones price, due to a buyer's inability to adequately assess its condition. She heeded my advice and was able to have it cleaned out for a proper sale. Be sure to revisit Chapter 4 for additional advice on decluttering your home.

Furnishings

Are your furnishings dated and obsolete? Occasionally I will tour a home and be overcome by a 1970's flashback because the home is full of orange or green shag carpet, flowery wallpaper, lots of wood paneling along with dated couches and chairs. Buyers often cannot see past the furniture and will associate it with the home, even though they are not included in the sale. It's best to remove dated carpet and furniture so buyers can be more objective about the home itself and not have their impressions tainted by its furnishings. Wallpaper can be another big turnoff, since many buyers know how labor intensive it is to remove. Unless you want a bare bones price for your property, you should be prepared to have some work done.

It's important you review all of the possibilities why your home is not selling, because time is not on your side.

The longer your home sits, the more days on market (DOM) it accrues, which will eventually lead to less showings and lower priced offers as time marches on.

Weather

There is always the possibility that weather is playing a role in your home sale woes. Time and time again I have seen foul weather put the kibosh on homes sales. When conditions are cold, windy, dark and rainy, it puts a damper on buyers touring properties. On the other hand, when the weather is bright, sunny and mild, people are much more upbeat and feel better about themselves and want to go out and spend money. I know personally when the weather gets bad, I prefer to hunker down and stay put, hoping for a better day tomorrow.

Many agents store away their summer earnings for fear of a bad winter because they anticipate fewer home sales. Rain alone can keep buyers indoors, as I have witnessed while hosting open houses during rainstorms. If you are running into a patch of bad weather, it is very important to have your home brightly lit and ready to greet visitors.

Perhaps put on a pot of coffee or hot tea to fill the home with a pleasant aroma, along with some soft music. If buyers feel like staying, then they will feel like buying. Do what you can to make them feel welcome.

TIP: *I have seen sellers vacate their homes for showings, leaving behind lit candles along with active fires in the fireplace. I don't recommend leaving your property with any* *unattended flames in the house. One year my family was celebrating Thanksgiving at my brother's home when someone noticed the dining room tablecloth was on fire. Thankfully, we caught it in time and there was no major damage except to the tablecloth and some napkins. We determined that a burning candle wick had broken off the candle and had fallen onto the table while we were all in the kitchen cleaning up. No one's fault, but it could have had huge consequences if we had not caught it in time.*

Price

Probably the biggest reason a house is not selling is the simple fact that it is priced too high. Buyers do not see the value of the home at its current listed amount. For example, 789 Jack Benny Lane has been listed for 178 days for a price of $275,000. The house is in decent condition but is nothing spectacular. The comparison homes have sold, on average, within 75 days on the market for approximately $265,000 to $280,000. This indicates that the property is in the ballpark, but is most likely priced too high, since it has been on the market much longer than the sold homes. If the seller were to reduce the price by $25,000 to $250,000, would the property sell? Most certainly YES, because buyers and their agents would see the excellent value of the property in comparison to the other recently sold homes.

Which means there is a *sweet spot* somewhere between $250,000 and $275,000 where the buyer will still see value and the seller will not have to lose their shirt. In this scenario, I would suggest that the seller make a price adjustment to $270,000 or $269,900 to see if that will be enticing enough to attract a buyer. For additional information, see *Pricing your Home* in Chapter 12.

The seller's agent should notify everyone who's seen the property of the *Great New Price!* Oftentimes those same buyers still have not found a property and may now consider this one as a possibility due to the price reduction.

Other Common Reasons

- Seller is too restrictive with showing availability. (e.g. weekday showings between 4-6 p.m. with no weekend showings). You need to make your home available as often as possible. Buyers will still be touring other homes whether or not your house is available to be seen. If they find a property they like, they will submit an offer and yours may never get a chance to be considered.

- Sellers are not vacating the property and not giving the buyers enough alone time in their home. Purchasers need to be able to explore and envision themselves in your house. If their tour lacks privacy, they will not feel comfortable discussing various features about the home.

- Property is located on a busy road or near a commercial or industrial type of property. Many purchasers with small children will not consider these and it will limit your pool of buyers. Special pricing needs to be considered when marketing these types of homes.

- Too many needed repairs. Perhaps your property is better suited for a handyman type of buyer. If so, your property should be marketed accordingly and not overstated in your property description sheet. If buyers' expectations are too high when visiting, they may be turned off by its actual condition.

There is always the slim possibility that there are just no buyers in your area at this particular time. When I was a teen, I liked to go fishing with my friends. There were days when we threw the line into the water and would instantly attract and catch lots of fish. There were other times when we would not even get a nibble. Why was that? We were fishing in the same spots, with the same bait, at the same time of day. Had all of the fish in the river gone fishing?

Sometimes there are just no takers. Timing is everything and there is the possibility that you may put your sign in the yard at a time when the fish just aren't biting.

Another possibility is you are not offering enough incentives to real estate agents to show and sell your home. It's important to know what the customary fees are in your area so know where to set yours to ensure that you get your fair share of interest.

Don't get discouraged, because I have some great ideas in the next chapter, where I will provide you with a list of incentives you can use to entice house hunters into taking the bait. Buyers love incentives, so be sure to use them to your advantage. Meet me on the next page for a friendly game of *Let's Make a Deal!*

Chapter 19

Top 10 Buyer Incentives

"Call it what you will,
incentives are what get people to work harder.
~Nikita Khrushchev

There are many different incentives you can offer that will entice buyers to purchase your home and also attract buyers' agents to sell your home. I will review some I have found to be particularly effective. However, if your market is red hot, it's doubtful you will need any incentives to sell your property. We will focus on the following enticements and discuss them in detail in this chapter.

Top Ten

1. Home Warranties
2. Appliance Packages
3. Window Treatments
4. Money towards Buyer's Closing Costs
5. Pool Memberships

6. Entertainment Systems
7. Lawn Equipment / Landscape Contracts
8. Association Dues / Condo Fees
9. Handyman / Cleaning Service
10. Agent Bonus

Home Warranties

Home warranties are a nice perk, especially for first-time homebuyers who are seeing their budgets stretched to the maximum and who are vulnerable to spikes in their expenses such as costly home repairs. This can be a wonderful add-on because the buyer's only risk is paying a small deductible of around $100 should something go wrong with the home within the first year. The warranty company will take care of the rest after the deductible is paid. Sellers will usually be covered under the warranty during the listing period, so be sure to ask.

Another nice feature of the home warranty is it eliminates phone calls to you about things that are going wrong with the home. For example, if the house you just sold has a roof leak within the first couple of months, I can practically guarantee that the buyer's agent will be calling your agent, who is going to be calling you, to inquire about what you know about the current roof leak. This is not the kind of rest and relaxation you're looking for after you sell your property.

However, if you purchased a home warranty, the chain of events would go more like this: Buyer contacts buyer's agent and informs her of a roof leak. Buyer's agent asks buyers if they called the home warranty company and reminds them that this is covered under the warranty and that they need to call the warranty company right away. Your listing agent's phone doesn't ring, and you hear nothing about the problem because it has been diverted to the warranty company. This peace of mind only costs around $500 and can not only help you sell the home but can alleviate future aggravating phone calls.

On one of my early investment properties I sold it without a home warranty and within weeks of closing I received a call from the buyer's agent informing me that the shower was leaking and the buyer was not pleased. Since I had rehabbed the property, I felt responsible and contacted my general contractor, who went out and fixed the problem.

All total, it took about a dozen phone calls and some minor worrying on my part. I would have much preferred to be out of the loop and not have to deal with any of it. From then on, I included a free home warranty on every home I sold and have not had a phone call since. So, the first, most basic incentive is to include a free home warranty.

Appliance Packages

Many first-time home buyers will not own a washer/dryer or refrigerator and will be elated if they are going to be included with the sale of the home. One of the first questions buyers ask me when touring a property is, "What is included with the sale of this home?" It is usually the larger appliances that they have their eye on because they know how costly they can be.

Sellers often don't realize their existing appliances will not be a good fit in their future home. Size and style can be way off.

A large, two-door refrigerator is not going to fit the *less is more* condo lifestyle into which they are moving.

This is a great time to market your appliances as included with the sale. Oftentimes appliances are also covered under a home warranty.

TIP: *I always recommend adding the following clause to all inclusions: All inclusions are in "as-is" condition. Meaning, the inclusions are a bonus for which you will not be responsible for replacing should any of them decide to break down before settlement. Without this clause, you could be buying a new large appliance, such as a refrigerator, to replace the deceased one.*

Window Treatments

If you haven't had to purchase curtains, rods, blinds, or window treatments in a while, consider yourself lucky. Not only are most of them expensive, but they are a pain to have to measure and install in your home. Buyers would prefer not to have to worry about this until they are better situated, which is why window treatments make for such a wonderful inclusion.

Chances are that your window treatments are not going to fit in your new home anyway, so you may as well leave them in place for the new homeowner.

When we were selling our last home, I asked my wife if we could leave all the window treatments with the sale so we could market it with this popular inclusion. She was adamant that this was not an option, since she had made most of them and thus they had sentimental value.

Being a believer of the *happy wife, happy life* philosophy, I backed off and excluded them with the purchase of our home. Years later, those same precious window treatments are adorning the crawlspace of our current home, stuffed in cardboard boxes. I've always wanted to say, "I told you so," but I'm smart enough to not go there. Still, the lesson is clear-only exclude window treatments if you know they will fit and where they will go in your next property. If you are uncertain, leave them for the enjoyment of the new owners. They will appreciate not having to mess with them the first month of ownership, especially since there are so many other projects that need to be completed. Thankfully, our home sold quickly, so there was no harm, no foul. ☺

TIP: *Make sure you put signs on special items you intend to leave so purchasers know they are included while touring your home. For example, you should tape a colorful sign to your entertainment system saying,* **Included with Home Sale!** *This can really get them visualizing how much fun it will be watching movies on the big screen in their great new home.*

Money Toward Closing Costs

As previously stated, money gets tight for buyers purchasing their first home, and even their second, which is why money toward closing costs is a very nice perk to offer. When buyers calculate all of the expenses in buying a home, including down payments, transfer taxes, legal fees, inspections, insurance, lender fees, title fees, etc., it can be daunting to see how much, if-any, is left over. For this reason, buyers love getting a portion of their closing costs paid at settlement. In my area, it is not uncommon to see sellers pay anywhere from 1% to 3% of the sale's amount toward the buyer's closing costs. Buyers of more expensive homes are not as likely to request or receive settlement assistance. In a vibrant seller's market, there will be less buyers seeking money toward closing costs unless absolutely necessary.

In offering this incentive up front, you will attract buyers who won't know if this money would otherwise be available without taking the time and effort to write a purchase offer. This can entice them to see your home, since competing properties may not be offering incentives.

Your property description and marketing should state something such as: *Seller will pay up to 2% of the purchase price towards buyer's closing costs with an acceptable offer.* Worded this way, you do not have to include all of it, should the offer not be what you expected. Chances are the buyers will be asking for settlement help anyway, so you may as well get some added marketing out of it.

Pool Memberships

Some developments have community pools into which neighbors can buy with the purchase of a pool bond and yearly membership fee. Neighborhood pools are especially nice because kids can walk or ride their bikes to the pool and don't need to be driven by their parents. If the community in which you live has a community pool, or if there is a pool not far away, it makes a wonderful incentive to get buyers thinking about how nice it would be to have this luxury so close to their future home.

Growing up, our family belonged to a community pool and my friends and I would ride our bikes practically every day to hang out, swim, play ping pong and eat ice cream. Our parents also loved it because it freed up their summers to do as they pleased, knowing we were in a protected environment with adult supervision.

Providing a free pool membership may rekindle your buyer's childhood memories of the neighborhood pool. This is a wonderful perk if you have a swim club nearby.

Entertainment Systems

Home entertainment systems are very popular these days with flatscreen TV's ranging anywhere from 46" to 86" wide. Many set ups also include surround sound speakers and movie-type seating. Entertainment systems can be difficult to move, and some sellers see this as a great way to leave their current set up in place as well as provide an incentive to purchase their home.

Your used flat screen TVs may be worth a lot more to your potential buyer than it is to you, so why not consider it as an incentive? This way you won't have to move any of that sensitive electrical equipment and can purchase an entirely new system with the proceeds from your sale. Consider this a good purchase incentive with an acceptable offer.

TIP: *Lenders do not like to see lots of inclusions or incentives written into the Agreement of Sale because it gives the appearance that the buyers are paying for these in the purchase price and are thus financing them. These same inclusions could negatively impact the home's appraisal if the appraiser works them into the purchase price. You may want to consider reviewing this with your agent, the loan originator or settlement attorney to determine the best course of action.*

Lawn Equipment / Landscaping Contracts

One of the many things a new homebuyer is not looking forward to is cutting and maintaining the lawn. I speak from experience on this point, having cut grass since I was around twelve years old. Buyers already have lots on their plate, including transferring utilities, unpacking boxes, finding lost items, tending to their kids, meeting new neighbors and learning a whole new routine.

If you cut your grass, it is a wonderful idea to include your lawn mower, gas cans and trimmer to go with the home. I have seen buyers drool over a seller's lawn equipment, hoping they can keep it. Buyers will overlook certain adverse issues of a home, knowing they are getting some cool inclusions. Why not get some marketing value up front for the landscaping equipment? This will be one last thing a buyer needs to worry about when you include yours with the sale of your property. If there's a chance you won't be doing the lawn work at your new place, you will surely get more value by adding the lawn equipment as an inclusion than you would trying to sell it secondhand.

Occasionally, sellers will not cut their grass but will choose to have a landscape company take care of this year-round. They may also have this same company do snow removal in the colder months. Since lawn care is akin to drudgery, including this free service makes for a wonderful incentive to sell your home for maximum profit. An example would be: *Six months free lawncare and/or snow removal with an acceptable purchase offer!* Of course, this will need to be worded to fit the appropriate time of year, but you get the general idea. I like the sound of it, and I am not looking to purchase a home.

TIP: *If you don't originally include many of these items with the sale of your home, they can be used as wonderful bargaining chips later on. If there are minor home inspection issues the buyers want fixed that you don't want to deal with, you can negotiate and provide additional inclusions instead of the repairs. For example, instead of hiring a mason to replace portions of the sidewalk, provide the purchaser with your riding lawn mower that you don't need anyway. Look for win-win situations.*

Homeowners Association Dues - Condo Fees

Most neighborhoods have homeowners' associations (HOA) that govern things like cutting common area grass such as the little islands in between streets, or at the neighborhood entrance, along with paying for the streets to be plowed in the winter months. Sometimes these fees are mandatory (meaning if you don't pay, they can attach liens to your home), or voluntary, in which everyone is expected to pay, but not required to pay. I've seen HOA dues cost anywhere between $50 to $750 per year. Including one year of HOA dues is a wonderful inclusion with your home because it will alleviate the buyer from having to deal with it until after they are settled in the next year.

Properties deeded as condominiums have common areas such as the clubhouse, swimming pool, an exercise facility, game rooms, hallways, etc., that require upkeep and maintenance. Depending on the size of the unit and what is covered, condo fees range anywhere from $150 per month to as high as $1,200 per month.

One of the first questions I often get when touring a condominium with a buyer is, "How much is the monthly condo fee?" If the amount is high, the buyer may want to abandon the tour, knowing what an extra burden this cost can be.

Offering an incentive such as: *First three months of condo fees included,* can be attractive to a buyer, as can, *First year of HOA fees included.* Even smaller incentives are a bonus that can grab a buyer's attention and differentiate your property from the competition.

Handyman / Cleaning Service

Buyers know they will have lots do to within the first few months of home ownership and would love to have a hand in doing them. Hiring a handyman for a day can be a wonderful perk to give to a buyer and to use in your marketing materials. This is probably better suited to homes in need of some TLC. However, new homeowners will still need pictures hung, furniture arranged and walls touched up, etc.

I honestly don't know of anyone who likes to clean house. Even my mother, who is the most immaculate housekeeper I have ever known, admits she does not like cleaning house and now has someone do it for her. When you get right down to it, many of us abhor housecleaning. However, many of those same people love and enjoy living in a clean house. It is simply the act of doing the work that we despise.

Since so many people hate to clean house, offering three-to-six months of free housekeeping to a buyer is a wonderful perk and one less thing for them to have to worry about during their initial months in their new home. It is an incentive I rarely see and yet it seems like such a no-brainer.

Depending upon where you are in your sales process, you can determine how much cleaning you are willing to pay for the new buyers. An enticement such as this can be cheaper than having to reduce the price a couple of times. Make sure you consider this much hated chore as an incentive to maximize the sale of your home.

Agent Bonus

I put this incentive last because it is the least liked by sellers. This bonus is often overlooked and can be downright frowned upon by sellers, which is understandable. I will hear them say, "I am already compensating the buyer's agent, why would I want to give them even more money," which is a valid argument. Here is the thinking process behind it. First of all, this does not have to be an incentive you use from

Day One, but it can be implemented if your home does not sell right away. Instead of dropping the sales price by $5,000 or $10,000 increments, provide a $1,500 bonus to the agency who brings an acceptable offer.

For example, say you are paying a 5% total commission with 2.5% being specified to the buyer's agent's side. There may be other property owners who are providing 3% to the buyer's agent's side of the commission, which makes your home less attractive to buyer's agents from the start.

When you provide an agent bonus, the agent most likely will not have to split this bonus with their broker. So, if you are giving a $1,500 agent bonus to the agent who brings the buyer, the agent's commission may now exceed a 3% buyers commission.

For example, 1422 East Main Street is for sale at $200,000 and is offering a 2.5% buyers broker commission that equals $5,000. If Realtor® Jerry Rice brings the winning bidder, he will need to split 50% of this commission with his broker, XYZ Real Estate. Jerry's total commission would be only $2,500.

Comparatively, 1502 Ormond Road is for sale at $200,000 and is offering a 3% buyers broker commission that equals $6,000. If Jerry brings the winning bidder to this property, he will receive $3,000 after his 50% split with XYZ Real Estate.

However, if 1422 East Main Street offers a $1,000 selling bonus on top of the 2.5% buyers broker commission, Jerry would earn $3,500, since he does not have to split the bonus with XYZ Real Estate. In short, both homes end up paying the same amount in commissions. However, 1422 East Main Street is now more attractive to buyer's agents because they will have the opportunity to earn additional money. Thus, you are getting more bang for your buck and agents will be attracted to show and sell your home first.

The beauty about this type of incentive is that you can remove it at any time. For example, if you drop your price from $330,000 to $325,000, it would be foolish to change the amount back to $330,000 if the property doesn't sell within the next 30 days, since it would negatively impact the sale. However, when utilizing an agent bonus, you could easily remove it with a time limitation. You are not bound to it should it not work out or if you change your mind.

I have successfully used the agent bonus to sell personal properties that were not selling quickly enough for me (remember the holding costs I discussed earlier). The money will simply come out of your closing proceeds; cash will not come out of your pocket before closing. It doesn't cost a lot to get agents interested in showing and selling your home first, versus the dozens of other homes also for sale.

Another advantage is that the buyer's agent is less likely to want the deal to fall apart should things go wrong during the inspections. Best to have them wanting things to work out, rather than having them want to cut bait and run away with their buyers to start touring homes again.

These are only a handful of incentive ideas. There are many others, including a one-year home security plan, a one-year health club membership, a golf membership, one year of movie passes for two, etc. Get creative and incentivize your home for maximum profit. Don't prejudge any of these incentives when selling your home for maximum value.

In the next chapter, I will review how to analyze incoming offers so you can easily differentiate the good, the bad and the ugly. I will also give you some valuable tips for unmasking buyer information. Grab your magnifying glass and meet me in on the following page!

PART VI:
DOCUMENTS REVIEW

Chapter 20

Analyzing Offers like a Professional

"Inaccurate analysis produces faulty insights and bad decisions, which leads to losing a tremendous amount of money."
~Stephen A. Schwarzman

   Many different components that make up an offer. It is important to pay attention to all of them and not just focus on price. For starters, real estate offers need to be in writing and signed by the buyers and sellers. Verbal contracts are not good enough. So, the first detail is to get everything in writing.

Here are the key components to an offer:

 ➤ Purchase Price
 ➤ Pre-Approval Letters
 ➤ Earnest Money Deposit

> ➤ Settlement Date
> ➤ Types of Financing
> ➤ Cash

Purchase Price

The highest purchase price is ultimately what we are looking for. However, just because the purchase price is the highest doesn't mean it's the best offer. My grandfather the lawyer would frequently say, "The big print gives it to you, the little print takes it away." He was referring to the way advertising will offer something in big print like, *Free Dinner for Two*, only to tell you somewhere in the small print that you have to *purchase a time share* to get your supposedly "free meal."

Real estate offers often mimic this sentiment because the generous purchase price can look very attractive-until you dig deeper and realize the buyers are asking for *6% settlement help and their purchase is contingent upon the sale of their current home.* Doesn't sound so wonderful now, does it?

One of the first things I do when receiving an offer is to print out a copy and review it with a yellow marker. I will circle the areas of the offer that I like, such as an amount equal to or above full price and will highlight in bold the areas of the contract for which I don't care for. I will also underline areas that need explaining by the buyer's agent. For example, often there will be blanks left in the contract that should not be ignored, such as the loan to value ratio (LTV), that tells you what percentage of the purchase price the buyer is borrowing from the lender. This is good to know this because you are better off with a lower LTV, since it means the purchaser is financing less and has more cash on hand should something go wrong, such as a low appraisal.

I will then contact the buyer's agent to get my questions answered and find out anything I else I can about the buyers, such as their employment and background information. I will also ask if this is going to be their primary residence. Do they have a house to sell, etc.? I will then paraphrase the offer on a piece of paper and email it so the sellers can easily see the meat and potatoes of the contract, and then I arrange to either meet with them in person or discuss it over the phone. I review everything with them and inform them of the good, the bad and the ugly.

While they are going over the offer terms and conditions, I will do some detective work to make sure that everything else is satisfactory. Back in the seller's market of 2003-2006, the market was crazy hot, and buyers' agents would do or say practically anything to get their offers accepted. For example, they would say that the purchase was not contingent upon a buyer's home sale when in fact it was. It was not uncommon to see pre-qualification letters that were overblown in the buyer's favor and omitted important information. Old habits die hard, so it's best to dig in and validate the offer as best as you can.

TIP: *Practically all purchase offers with financing will be contingent upon the buyer's ability to obtain a mortgage, with the guarantee that their earnest money will be refunded to them if they are unable to procure the loan. This typically occurs during the latter part of the transaction, which is why*

it's vitally important to obtain as much information as
possible to avoid the deal falling through.

Pre-Approval Letters

I then focus on the pre-approval letter that was submitted
with the contract. Is the financial lending institution a
national brick and mortar company such as *Wells Fargo*, or
are they primarily an Internet loan service like *Rocket
Mortgage*, or a lesser known internet lender such as
lendup.com? It's usually best to have the purchaser use a
known, established lender that is no stranger to your area. I
have found some online lenders to be hard to deal with due
to their poor communications.

I will then call the loan officer to verify the accuracy
of the pre-approval letter and review the buyer's
qualifications. It's important to ensure the buyer is able to
purchase your home and thus prevent a dreaded
cancellation later. Loan officers work on a commission basis.
They, too, want the deal to go through so they can earn a
paycheck. They will often inform me of just how much work
they have done to pre-approve their client, which can
include running a full-blown credit check from the three
credit agencies (Equifax, Experian and Transunion) and
verifying assets, employment and income. Sometimes
lenders will only run the purchaser's credit from one agency,
and they may miss valuable information from the other two
credit agencies.

TIP: *Kevin Hollerman, sales manager with **Movement
Mortgage** says, "The lender letter should never say **pre-***

qualification. It should only say **pre-approval.** *" He also states, "The home seller should ask their listing agent to call and inquire with the loan officer about the strength of the buyer's file as soon as possible. "*

I will also ask if the buyer needs settlement help to close. For example, if the buyer is asking for 5% settlement help on a $300,000 purchase price, that amounts to $15,000 in financial assistance that the seller will have to provide them at closing. I want to know if the buyers merely want it or need it to close. I can usually get the lender to tip their hat and provide me with important information which will prove useful in drawing up a counteroffer.

If the seller's assistance is not mandatory for the buyer to obtain their financing, I may be able to prevent the seller from giving away too much of their hard-earned equity. If buyers merely want settlement help, the amount can most likely be negotiated lower.

Lastly, I will ask if the purchase is contingent upon the sale of any current real estate. The bottom line is this: I don't want to tie up the house for a month or two only to find out a few days before settlement that the buyers can't close due to their current home sale falling through. The more that can be done upfront to qualify an offer, the better the probability that the deal will go through.

Once I've determined they are good and capable buyers, I double check to see if they have a house to sell. I start by researching the home address they listed on the *Agreement of Sale.* Do they own this property or are they renting it? If they are renting, that is a good sign, since they most likely don't have a house to sell. If they do own the home, I will check and see if it is currently for sale via the MLS or as a FSBO, or see if it is being marketed as a rental.

If it is not for sale, I will research how much money is owed on it and approximately what the current value is. It is useful to know how much equity they have in the home should they need some cash to close. If it is mortgaged to the hilt, that is not a good sign, although not necessarily a deal breaker.

Remember, *knowledge is power.* The more I can find out about this buyer and their financial wherewithal, the better chance the seller and I have of walking to the promised land (settlement table). Additionally, if competing offers come in, I will be able to compare this data side-by-side to help the seller choose the smarter offer.

Earnest Money Deposit - EMD

So far, so good. Now it's time to review some of the contract's other important details, such as the *earnest money deposit.* The EMD is the amount of upfront money the buyer is providing along with their purchase contract. It is typically held by a title company or the listing broker's escrow account. In general, the EMD shows the buyer's commitment to the deal. For example, if the good faith deposit is $5, it means the purchasers can walk away at any time during the transaction and only lose $5. If you were the seller, how confident would you be in this buyer completing the transaction? Not very!

Conversely, if the buyer puts down a deposit of $10,000, it is much more of a commitment to buy. Keep in mind, the EMD is typically refundable if any of the home sale contingencies go awry. For example, if the purchaser makes the purchase contingent upon the home not having radon and the radon test fails, then they would be entitled to get their money back. Typically, the EMD is not refundable if the buyer merely changes their mind.

In short, the EMD is not exactly money in the bank. However, I still like to see it amount to at least 1.5% of the purchase price. For example, if the purchase price is $300,000, I like to see the EMD to be at least $4,500. I would prefer 2-3%, especially if the buyer is borrowing 80% or less, because they have more cash on hand verses buyers who are financing higher amounts such as 95%. Homes with fewer days on market and lots of buyer interest should be looking for a higher EMD.

Settlement Date

The settlement date is important because it needs to fit the seller's timeline and ideally should not be further out than 60 days from the date the contract was signed by both parties, unless the seller prefers to wait longer.

Why? Because, the further out the settlement date is, the more time there is for things to go wrong. The more things that go wrong, the higher the probability that the deal will fall apart. The longer the wait time, the better chance there is for a buyer job loss, death in the family, divorce, squandered funds, change of heart, etc.

Consequently, the shorter time between the signed offer and the settlement date, the less chance of anything bad happening, provided they can secure the loan in time.

In my real estate career, I have experienced the following events while under contract with clients:

- Death of a spouse (deal delayed, but salvaged)
- Buyer lost all of his down payment money (deal lost)
- Big tree fell the day before closing (deal salvaged)
- Buyer didn't like home anymore (deal lost)
- Parents didn't like home (deal salvaged)
- Heart attack (deal lost)

As you can see from my own experiences, sh*t really does happen. The longer amount of time you allow until settlement, the better chance that something unfavorable is going to occur. If you don't like the date the buyer requests, make sure you negotiate to change it.

TIP: *I have witnessed sellers let their house go once they've accepted an offer. Doing so can have negative consequences to the buyers should they happen to pop in for some reason. Lastly, appraisers are also human (although some agents may argue this point) and may devalue the home if they feel the condition is lesser. Appraisers rarely give more than 24 hours' notice of a visit, so you'll want the place looking sharp at all times. They, too, can get negative vibes from a dirty, unkempt house.*

Types of Financing

There are many different types of financing and they are not all created equal, as some are preferred by agents and sellers more than others. Certain types of financing can require sellers to "jump through hoops" much more than others, so you must be knowledgeable about them so you don't find yourself performing in a circus act.

The types of financing that you may encounter are:

- ➤ Conventional
- ➤ Federal Housing Administration (FHA)
- ➤ United States Department of Veterans Affairs (VA)
- ➤ United States Department of Agriculture (USDA)
- ➤ Seller Financing
- ➤ Cash

Conventional Financing

The most common and easiest loan for sellers to deal with is a conventional loan. This can range anywhere from 50% loan to value (LTV), up to 95% LTV. It is the least restrictive regarding a home's current condition in comparison to other consumer loans.

Most banks, credit unions and mortgage companies provide conventional financing. As long as the home's major systems are in working order, the property is free of leaks and has no noticeable major defects, conventional financing should be easy to obtain, provided the buyer qualifies.

This type of loan is also the least expensive for buyers, since conventional interest rates are typically lower and offer flexible terms regarding repayment. For purchasers to qualify, they will need above average credit scores along with solid earnings.

If a borrower finances more than 80% of the purchase price, purchasers will be required to pay for private mortgage insurance (PMI). This can be eliminated once home equity equals 20% or more of the value of the house.

TIP: *When receiving multiple offers, special attention should be given to conventional financing with low loan to value ratios, for example, if the buyer is borrowing only 80% or less of the purchase price. This type of financing is considered more stable because the purchaser has more skin in the game due to less money being financed. Don't just get hung up on the highest price, since there is added benefit to buyers with more cash on hand and less financial risk of having their loan denied and your closing delayed which can cost you money.*

The Federal Housing Administration - FHA

FHA insured loans are backed by the Federal Housing Administration which is part of the U.S. Department of Housing and Urban development (HUD). FHA does not make loans but insures loans made by an FHA approved lending institution. FHA loans are popular because they will lend a high percentage of the purchase price, up to 96.5%, which means the buyer only needs to come up with 3.5% of the purchase price, not including closing costs. FHA is very popular with first time homebuyers and will also allow a purchaser to receive up to 6% settlement assistance from the seller.

For example, your house sells for $200,000 and you agree to provide the purchaser with 3% closing assistance, or $6,000; with the buyers loan of $193,000 ($200,000 x .965), minus the $6,000 settlement help, the buyer only needs to come up with an additional $1,000 ($7,000 - $6,000) plus closing costs, (attorney fees, title insurance, transfer taxes, home owners insurance, etc.)

This is a popular loan choice for purchasers that have not saved a lot of money because it allows them to finance a greater percentage of the home's purchase price. The one downside to FHA is it requires mortgage insurance protection (MIP) to be paid every month for the life of the loan. Whereas previously discussed, conventional loans mortgage insurance (PMI) can be halted when equity reaches 20% of the home's value.

NOTE: *A little known seller benefit of an FHA loan is that the mortgage can be assumed by a buyer, provided they meet FHA guidelines. This makes your home more marketable if you currently have an FHA loan and your mortgage interest rate is attractive. Most conventional mortgages cannot be assumed by a buyer.*

A downside of FHA loans for sellers is that they require the appraisal to be done by an FHA, HUD certified appraiser, who will also be inspecting the home for safety hazards such as the lack of handrails, trip hazards, heaving sidewalks, driveways or patios, and evidence of peeling paint inside or outside of the home.

The difference between these repair items and typical home inspection repair requests, is that FHA repairs are mandatory and need to be completed before closing. Once the appraisal repairs have been completed the appraiser will be notified to go back out and review the finished work. If they have not been completed to the appraiser's satisfaction, settlement will not occur until they are done.

I once had a pesky FHA appraiser reinspect my seller's paint repairs three times before he would authorize the work. This is not typical of most FHA deals. As a seller, you will not want to consider FHA financing if your home needs a fair amount of work.

FHA 203K

FHA 203K sounds like a retirement vehicle but it is a type of rehab financing which enables a buyer to purchase a home that would otherwise be unfinanceable without prior repairs. Just like FHA loans, FHA 203K insured loans are backed by the Federal Housing Administration.

The approved lender will establish an estimated repair cost and provide financing on that amount, along with the cost to purchase the home, so the buyer can close on the property and then repair the home using lender-approved contractors.

For example, Archie Baker purchases 704 Houser Street, a foreclosure property he bought through the bank via a 203K loan. The current value of the house is approximately $100,000. After a new roof, a new kitchen and some new windows, the house will be worth around $195,000.

The lender will loan the money to buy the house ($100,000) and will then provide the rehab funds ($65,000) to the purchaser in installments, as long as the bank receives verification that the work is being done and Archie is not spending the money at the local casino. Once the work is completed and the contractors are all paid, Archie ends up with a house worth approximately $195,000, for which he only paid a total of $165,000 plus closing costs, netting him approximately $30,000 in equity.

FHA 203K is a great way to market and sell unfinanceable properties. If not for this option, they would have to be sold to investors who want to pay the absolute bare minimum for properties using cash funds. You've seen the signs *Cash for your Home.* Yes, there will be no financing involved, but it won't even be close to maximizing your home's value. They are purchasing it to rehab it and maximize its equity for themselves.

A good friend of mine purchased a wonderful ranch house via FHA 203K financing and had it fixed up into a very warm and inviting home. He says it was a hassle dealing with the lender throughout all the repairs, but was well worth it in the end, especially since he's now sitting on a good chunk of home equity.

In short, if your home needs a lot of major repairs, FHA 203K financing may be the only way for you to attract a buyer willing to pay a reasonable price. I have seen foreclosure properties and estate sales successfully transacted utilizing this type of financing. This is most likely going to net you more proceeds than selling your home for cash to a real estate investor.

United States Department of Veterans Affairs - VA

A VA guaranteed loan is a mortgage loan on an approved property made to a qualified veteran by an authorized lender and guaranteed by the U.S. Department of Veterans Affairs to limit the lender's possible loss. VA loans offer 100%

financing to active military and retired veterans in good standing. They also allow up to 6% settlement assistance. I have witnessed veterans receive money back at closing due to the generous financing and settlement assistance from the seller. VA financing, like FHA loans, requires mortgage insurance (MIP) for the life of the loan.

VA appraisals must be performed by a VA certified appraiser who will also be inspecting the home for safety hazards, similar to the FHA appraiser. VA financing is a wonderful way for veterans to purchase a home with very little out-of-pocket expenses.

NOTE: *VA loans can also be assumed by a qualified buyer, which make them advantageous when selling during periods of rising interest rates.*

United States Department of Agriculture - USDA

The first time I heard of USDA loans, I thought to myself, "Aren't they the ones who grade our beef?" USDA loans are issued through the USDA loan program that assists approved lenders in providing low to moderate income households the opportunity to own housing in eligible areas as their primary residences.

Approved lenders can offer 100% financing with low interest rates to qualified purchasers. The properties need to be in a certain predefined area which is outlined on their website maps. Visit https://eligibility.sc.egov.usda.gov/ to see if your address is located in one of these areas. If it is, your home may have added value due to its liberal financing options through USDA, where buyers have less stringent lending requirements and will need less of their own funds to purchase.

USDA appraisals need to be performed by HUD certified appraisers and have similar requirements as FHA appraisals, meaning, the appraiser will also be inspecting the home for similar safety hazards and peeling paint.

A former client of mine would only look at USDA area homes because of their excellent terms. We found a real beauty that was bank owned that he was able to purchase with a USDA loan and that allowed him to finance 100% of the property.

When I presented the offer to the listing agent, he had no idea the house was located in an approved USDA area. He confided with me later that had he known it was when he listed the property, he would have marketed it as such, and thought it would have sold much quicker and for more money than it did.

Seller Financing

If you can purchase a home without selling your existing property and your debt is paid off with the lender, you can consider offering owner financing, where you will play the role of the financial institution. Providing financing can help you attract more buyers and has the potential of boosting your sales price. I don't recommend seller financing if your current loan is not paid off. That topic would be better discussed with your financial adviser.

You will want to ensure that the buyer is well-qualified to purchase your home, since you will be holding the note, and monthly payments will be going directly to you.

Seller financing works as follows: You list your home for sale at a set price, notifying the purchaser that you will hold financing. Buyers and their agents will present purchase offers as they normally would, only this time they are not going to be applying with lenders for financing, but with you. The buyers should be pre-approved by a mortgage lender to ensure their ability to purchase your home. Chances are they have already established a relationship with a lender before searching for homes.

If you decide to provide owner financing, you will need to inform the buyer of the specific lending terms, i.e. interest rate, length of loan, etc. Make sure you have your attorney write up all of the necessary documents. If the buyer agrees, you will proceed to sign all of the necessary paperwork approved by your attorney.

NOTE: *Not all states are mortgage states that allow the lender to place a lien on the property should the buyer default. Some states use a Trust Deed, which is a legal instrument used to create a lien on a property. Be sure to ask your local real estate attorney which instrument is commonplace in your area so you will be able to re-acquire the house should the buyer default.*

Once all of the home purchase commitments have been satisfied, you will head to closing. The buyers will then sign a note promising to repay the loan. They will also be signing either a mortgage document or deed of trust that will provide you with collateral should they default on their payments. This will allow you to reclaim the property should they stop making payments. You are now playing the role as a lender normally would, since the monthly payments will now be going to you.

Seller financing is much more popular in slower real estate markets when homes aren't selling, and owners can get creative to get them sold. By offering financing, they can offer generous terms and low interest rates to help sell their property. I have not had many buyers or sellers partake in this type of financing.

Cash

Although a cash purchase is not financed, it deserves honorable mention because of the simple fact that *Cash is King!* The beauty of cash is that there is no need to have an appraisal done unless the purchaser specifically requests it.

Without lender financing, there is no jumping through hoops trying to satisfy the lender. If you are presented with a cash offer, make sure you ask the buyers or their agent for a recent *Proof of Funds* letter provided by their financial institution, documenting that they have the available cash proceeds in their account. I have seen purchasers say they can pay with all cash funds when they do not have the money in their possession, because they are waiting for a legal settlement, lottery proceeds, etc. Trust but verify that these funds are available so you're not wasting valuable time on a deal that may never close.

Most likely you will not receive as much money with a cash offer due to its convenience and the increased certainty of closing. Provided the disparity is not too great, it may be worth the loss of some equity due to the added benefits, along with a quick closing, since you are only waiting for inspections and title work to be done and the transference of the deed without waiting for a loan approval. I have seen cash deals close in as quickly as ten days. Love it!

In summary, it's important you review the type of financing the purchaser will be applying for, since it can determine how smoothly your transaction goes. Different situations, such as the condition of your home, along with the buyer's financial wherewithal, will determine the best type of financing for your property. Be sure to ask questions if you think the type of loan for which they are applying is less than suitable for your home.

In the next chapter, I will be reviewing likely property inspections the purchaser will conduct on your home. It's essential that you are familiar with them so you will be in a better position to negotiate when the buyers submit their request for repairs. Grab a flashlight and let's get started!

Chapter 21

Home Inspections

"When it comes to privacy and accountability, people always demand the former for themselves and the latter for everyone else."
~David Brin

This chapter is solely focused on home inspections, including:

> - Main Inspection
> - Inspection Reports
> - Estimated Repairs
> - Cash in Lieu of Repairs
> - Local Government Inspections

Home inspections can make or break a deal, so it's important to know as much about them as you can.
No one likes having their home prodded, poked and put under a microscope. Unfortunately, it is a necessary evil in selling real estate in the 21st Century. Believe it or not, many

buyers are almost as worried about the inspections as the sellers, because they don't want to see their beautiful dream home revealed as a poorly built money pit. Many sellers think that buyers are after their blood, but this is not usually the case, as they too are navigating in choppy, unknown waters.

Main Inspection

The biggest inspection is the one performed on the entire house. I don't think sellers should be present for this inspection. I have witnessed sellers who wish to stay home, only to find that it leads to confrontation, which is just not healthy for the relationship.

However, it is important that someone other than the buyer and home inspector attend the inspection. This should be the buyer's agent, but on numerous occasions I have seen where the purchaser's agent does not attend. If this is the case, then the listing agent should be at the home while it is being inspected so the buyers are not left alone in the home without supervision of some kind.

The home inspector's job is to inspect the property. They will be far too busy performing their duties and won't know what the buyers are up to while they are working. Make sure you or your agent asks the buyer's agent if he or she is planning to attend the inspection. If not, ask that your agent be in attendance.

TIP: *Most lenders require a satisfactory Wood Destroying Insect Inspection (aka Termite Inspection) for the buyer to obtain their loan. Be sure to provide the buyer with any*

information on prior treatments or inspections. This will be
comforting to a buyer before their inspection, especially if
the inspector notes evidence of prior treatment during his
visit.

Most sales contracts mention that the purchaser is not
buying a new home and states that the purpose of the home
inspection is to point out major defects in the property,
along with any items that are not working as intended or
operating in an unsafe manner. For example, electrical
outlets in the kitchen and baths not being ground-fault circuit
interrupter protected (GFCI). Many contracts will also state
that the home inspection does not concern cosmetic items
such as scratches on a countertop or a small hole in an
interior wall, as they are not major defects but merely
superficial issues not within the scope of the inspection.

It is important to note that a home inspector is hired
by the buyer to point out deficiencies in the home they are
inspecting. I have witnessed many home inspectors trying to
impress buyers by demonstrating how much knowledge they
have regarding home construction and its relevant systems.
Sometimes they may appear happy to find deficiencies and
thus help justify their fees. In short, some tend to be
overzealous with their findings. It's an interesting
relationship, to say the least.

Having witnessed hundreds of home
inspections firsthand, some inspectors are much better than
others at presenting their clients with important information
regarding issues they've encountered. Seasoned and
knowledgeable inspectors will know how to present defects
to a buyer in the proper context, without scaring them into
thinking the issue is of greater concern than it is. For

example, if the inspector points out to his client that he noticed a little effervescence (moisture) coming through the block wall and that it needs to be corrected immediately, the buyer may be under the impression that this is severe, and start to feel badly about their purchase.

Consequently, if the home inspector merely informs them of the effervescence and states that it should be corrected, but also notes that it is very common in basements, the buyer would not be as alarmed and have a much better understanding of it. When purchasers are repeatedly given overblown inspection data, they become disillusioned into thinking they may have a lemon on their hands and begin thinking of exit strategies.

This is especially concerning with first time home buyers who are not used to many of the typical imperfections that can be present in a home. It is important to know what sort of buyers you have, so that when you critique the inspection reports you can get a better understanding of what their main concerns are and why.

Minor home inspection issues can be magnified to the point of scaring a buyer into not wanting to purchase the home, when all it needs is some minor repairs. A good home inspector knows how to spot problems in a house and put it into the proper context in which to explain them to a buyer.

A good example of a dire issue is the discovery of a cracked heat exchanger, where carbon monoxide is leaking into the home's air flow. This is a major issue and should be addressed as such, because of the severity of the problem and the large expense of having to replace the heater. I would expect a home inspector to point out the seriousness of this issue. Be sure to revisit Chapter 6 for additional information on testing for radon, water and lead.

Inspection Reports

Once the home inspections are completed, the inspector will send the reports to the buyer and buyer's agent, who will review them and write up a list of repairs on an *Endorsement to the Agreement of Sale* or *Inspection Addendum*. It will sound something like this: *Buyer and Seller agree that the Seller is responsible for making the following repairs using licensed contractors and providing the Buyer with the necessary receipts and warranties prior to settlement.* It will then list the needed repairs, such as: *Kitchen electrical outlets were not functioning at the time of inspection. Have licensed electrician review and replace as necessary.* The buyer's agent will have the buyer sign off on the endorsement and will forward it to the listing agent or seller if FSBO.

Typically, agents write into the sales agreement that the buyer will have approximately two weeks to provide the seller with any defects found in the inspection. The contract will then provide a few days for the seller to review and respond, with an additional couple of days added for both parties to agree. The specific timelines will all be spelled out in the purchase agreement.

As a seller's agent, one of the first things I do after reading a home inspection report, along with the request for repairs document, is to review the seller's disclosure to see if any of the requested repairs were disclosed upfront by the seller. If so, those repair requests should be off limits, since it was previously disclosed. I will then contact the buyer's agent and ask what the buyer's main concerns are regarding the property. This will often get them to reveal which repair requests are not important to the buyer. I'll also ask if the agent thinks the buyer would be okay with a credit instead of the repairs. This can save lots of time and energy if they are good with a money credit at closing.

With all of this information, I'll contact the seller and review the findings with them. We can often negotiate and agree to only fix what is necessary to appease the buyers, provided, of course, that the issues are actually major defects or valid safety concerns.

Estimated Repairs

If the buyers want estimates, I feel it is always in the seller's best interest to obtain their own estimates. Otherwise, the estimates could be padded with unnecessary extras which will increase the price of the repairs. For example, during a home inspection it is determined that you have a legitimate roof leak. The lazy listing agent doesn't feel like contacting anyone, so the buyer contacts his licensed roofer, who comes out and estimates the work at $9,075, stating that all of the existing shingles need to be removed and replaced with new 30-year architectural shingles.

If the listing agent was proactive and had experience in this area, he or she should probably know a contractor who specializes in roof repairs and could replace the defective area for around $325 and warranty the repair. Which would you rather pay? I have found many roofing contractors push for new roofs instead of repairs due to simple economics.

A good agent will be able to review the report and explain what is important and what is routine. Agents should have ongoing relationships with dependable, hardworking contractors who can promptly address these issues and provide timely free estimates. The bottom line is this: if the buyer still wants to buy and the seller still wants to sell, then there is nothing that can't be worked out between the two parties regarding the home inspection.

If you are in a tussle over the home inspection repairs, try and see it from the buyer's point of view. If their inspector told them the roof is awful and this is their first home purchase, how would you feel if you were in their shoes? Would you be thinking that it doesn't matter or would you be looking for some sort of restitution? Often, when we step in the other persons shoes, the view looks much different.

Also, make sure the listing agent paints an accurate picture of your side to the buyer's agent. For example, perhaps you just had the driveway redone and added all new fencing. Have your agent remind the buyer's agent that you have just spent a lot of money on the house and should be given some leeway.

Sometimes, simple negotiations can alleviate a problem between buyer and seller. I've seen sellers say they won't fix something because it wasn't an issue for them when they lived in the home, such as step cracks in exterior brick. The buyer asks for it to be repaired but agrees to a free home warranty instead of the repairs. It never hurts to offer different resolutions to an issue.

Cash in Lieu of Repairs

One of the easiest ways to put home inspection issues to bed is to offer the buyer a credit at settlement. This money will come out of the seller's proceeds and onto the buyer's side of the settlement sheet. For example: Seller says, *Seller will credit the buyer $500 at closing instead of any repairs.* The buyer will often take this option because they figure they may take a shot at fixing it themselves and keep the extra $500.

Providing cash instead of repairs also means the issue is now finished and over with. If you do decide to make repairs, you will need to provide the buyer with receipts, and they will be scrutinizing the work after it has been completed. I have seen buyers review work and say things like, "That color doesn't match. I want it done over." Or, "Why didn't they fix the entire crack and not just the worst part?"

In short, the work might not be done to their satisfaction and the issue may not be over with. This can create enormous headaches for everybody. Beauty is in the eye of the beholder and everyone can have a different opinion. Cash is cash and it will not change in complexity once everyone has agreed to it. This is what makes cash in lieu of repairs so neat, clean and easy.

However, sometimes the buyers will want to have their own estimates. If this is the case, be sure to get estimates using your contractors. If the buyer wants the money instead of the repairs, he should get the amount stated in the lowest of all the estimates. Once you do come to an agreement, it's important to put it in writing and have everyone sign it. Memories may get foggy, so don't leave it to chance.

States differ regarding inspections and if and when a purchaser is permitted to negate a contract due to home inspection findings. In some states, a seller has the opportunity to fix all of the legitimate home inspection repair requests and the buyer is still obligated to purchase the home, provided the repairs are completed as stated. In other states, buyers are permitted to walk away from a purchase agreement if they do not like any of the results uncovered by the home inspections. Be sure to check what your state laws require so you will know what your options are.

No matter where the home is located, if a buyer receives a non-satisfactory home inspection and is extremely disappointed in the results, the deal is doomed to fail, even if the seller agrees to correct the issues. Once the home loses its luster for a buyer, it will be difficult to keep them on board. The only other leverage the seller has is to refuse to sign over the earnest money deposit. If the deposit is a sizable amount, like $10,000, this can easily change a buyer's mind, as they won't want to throw away money for nothing.

As I have stated previously, issues with the home inspection are the number one reason for deals not closing. Inspections wreck more deals than low home appraisals or a buyer's inability to obtain financing combined. Special care and consideration need to be given to the home inspection report and repair requests so you can close on time and maximize your returns.

Local Government Inspections

It's important to note that some local governments or municipalities will require properties to be inspected before they can be sold to another party. This typically involves a local inspector to walk the property and ensure it is safe for occupancy. If repairs are needed, they will have to be completed for the property to close and transfer to the new owner. Be sure to check with local professionals and see what types of local inspections your property could be subjected to.

I have also seen home sales subject to the buyer's insurance company inspecting the property. This is a rare occurrence but it does happen. They appear particularly interested in reviewing a home's electrical components.

In the next chapter, I will discuss another real estate thorn that can send a deal spiraling out of control and cost you lots of money. Grab a cool drink along with some aspirin and meet me on the next page!

Chapter 22

Appraisal Anxiety

"It's not the load that breaks you down,
it's the way you carry it."
~Lou Holtz

There are two hurdles that can derail a real estate transaction faster than an Amtrak train. The first one is the home inspection, which we addressed in the previous chapter. The second equally deadly occurrence is the dreaded real estate appraisal. This can make or break a deal in no time, so there are things you should know and do to help ensure that your home appraises for the maximum.

Each U.S. State or territory has a State Appraiser Regulatory Agency that is responsible for certifying and licensing real estate appraisers and supervising their appraisal-related activities as required by federal law.

Form 1004

All residential appraisals are done on the same form, called the *Uniform Residential Appraisal Report Form 1004,* which is used nationwide. When an appraiser completes the form, they will arrive at one main value determined by using at least one of three methods.

Method 1: *Cost Approach,* or how much will it cost to rebuild the home should it be destroyed.

Method 2: *Comparison Approach,* or how much the home is worth in comparison to other similar homes in the same area.

Method 3: *Income Capitalization* approach, which is better suited for commercial income producing properties such as apartments, because it determines value based on the amount of income it produces, along with some other factors.

The method primarily used in residential appraisals is the comparison approach, which is what we will be focusing on. The process begins with an appraiser visiting your home to walk the property, take photos and record notes. They will also take measurements to determine the overall square footage of the house. Appraisers will compare your property to similar, nearby homes that have recently sold, are active on the market or are currently pending settlement. They will add or subtract value from the comparable properties' sold amount to determine a value for the subject property (house being sold).

For example, 11222 Dilling Street (subject property) is under contract and is being appraised by XYZ Appraisers, hired by the buyer's lending institution. When the appraisers compare the subject property to other recently sold homes, they notice that the sold properties all have screened porches, whereas 11222 Dilling Street has an enclosed glass porch which is an improvement over a screened porch. They will add an amount, such as $5,000, to the comparison home's sold price to place a value on the subjects improvement.

Suppose 11222 Dilling Street only has a one car garage, but several of the comparable sold homes have two car garages. The appraiser would then subtract approximately $5,000 from the sold two car garage homes' selling price in order to compensate for 11222 Dilling Street's lack of a second car garage. This will be done for all the various amenities and improvements between the subject property and the sold homes it is being compared to provide an apples-to-apples comparison.

Appraisers Visit

It is very important to have your listing agent meet the appraiser at the property to give him or her an overview of the home and provide a list of the improvements. When I am meeting with an appraiser, I always arrive early to make sure the temperature is at a comfortable setting and all the lights are on inside the home. I want it to look just as inviting as if the appraiser were a prospective home buyer.

This means the home should be in the same show-ready condition as it would be for an open house. All beds are made, and clothes are neatly put away. In the kitchen, dirty dishes are out of sight and appliances and countertops are free of crumbs and fingerprints. Toys are picked up and stashed away. Outside, the lawn is cut and any outdoor equipment is out of site. I understand you are in the process of moving and that this can be very difficult. It is okay to have filled boxes in some rooms. Just have them neatly pushed to one side. Try to maintain organization within the chaos.

Remember, the goal is to do everything within your power to make your home look especially nice so the appraiser feels your home's charm and values it at or above the sales amount. Because appraisers will be taking photos of practically every room in the home, it is to your benefit that the house looks good in the photos, because they may be reviewed by others affiliated in the appraisal process.

Sellers do not have to be present for the appraiser's visit. I prefer that the owners are not present, since they can be overly emotional about their home and emotions are not a part of the appraiser's calculations. However, as I mentioned previously, it is important that your agent be present to represent the property and prepare for the visit.

I typically greet the appraiser inside the home and thank them for being prompt. I let them know I turned on all of the lights for their convenience and tell them not to bother with turning them off and that I will take care of it. I will walk around the main level of the home, pointing out some of the major improvements, and then ask them if they have any questions. If they are chatty, I will continue with them for the remainder of the walkthrough. If they are more standoffish, I will simply review the major improvements and let them tour the home alone, reminding them that I am nearby should they have any questions.

When they are finished, I again ask if they have any questions and then hand them a packet of information enclosed in a sharp-looking professional folder that includes house data (e.g. home improvements), the property descriptions of comparable properties in the area that are for sale (pending and sold), along with my business card. I thank them for all of their efforts and ask them to feel free to reach out to me if they think of any questions or run into any problems. I walk them to the front door and see them out.

Ever since I started meeting with appraisers, I have not had any appraisal issues, except for minor FHA repairs (need a handrail, fix peeling paint, etc.). However, every one of those FHA appraisals came in at or above the purchase price, which is excellent.

I'm amazed at how many other agents don't take the additional steps for their seller or do everything possible to try and ensure that the appraisal process goes smoothly. I would estimate that only around 5% of real estate agents take the time to do this.

I can't say I relish the added step of meeting with the appraiser; however, I enjoy it much more than having to contact the seller with the grim news that the house appraised for less than the sales price!

TIP: *FHA appraisals are good for six months from the appraisal date. VA certified appraisals are good for 120 days from the appraisal date. If your home is under contract with any of the above financing and it appraises low and the deal falls apart, future FHA and VA lenders will be using the same appraisal report that derailed your prior deal until the* *length of time expires. However, you could resell your property with conventional financing and not be restricted to the prior appraisal because a new appraisal will be ordered for the conventional financing.*

Contesting a Low Appraisal

There is always a chance that things won't go as planned and the appraisal amount will come in below the selling price. When this occurs, some steps can be taken to try and rectify the situation. However, you will need overwhelming evidence that supports your argument that the process was done in error. This is not an easy task, so don't get your hopes up.

The first step is to get your hands on the appraisal, and have it reviewed by a professional who understands how to read and understand it. You'll want to double check and see if the comparable properties are of the same type, location, size and condition as your property. If not, then it is important that the correct adjustments have been made. You will also need to have access to the comparable homes' data so that can be reviewed.

If you are working with an agent, its best to have him or her review it with you. If it appears that you have a case, the agent should bring this to the manager of the agent's brokerage company for further review. If the manager feels it has been done in error, they can formulate a dispute letter explaining why they feel that an injustice has been done and submit the appeal to the lending institution that ordered the appraisal. The appraisal will then be reviewed and a decision will be rendered within approximately five business days.

I can count on one hand how many times I have witnessed having the value changed to a higher amount, which is not many. It is rare, but possible, so it's important to get as much information as you can to determine your next step. At least you will gain some insight as to why your house was valued the way it was.

Lastly, you can try and order another appraisal if the lending institution agrees. This may or may not work in your favor and you might receive pushback from the buyer. Be sure to have your agent discuss this option with the lender.

Knowing as much as you can about the appraisal process can help you better prepare for it. Leave nothing to chance and do all you can to ensure your home appraises to the max!

NOTE: *If appraisers are competent with determining the value of homes, why are they provided the selling price before they conduct their appraisals?*

Be sure to revisit Chapter 20 for a refresher on how FHA and VA financing can have more stringent home condition requirements than conventional financing.

In the next chapter, I will discuss some additional items on your to-do list which you will need to complete for you have a successful final walkthrough. You are getting close to the finish line!

PART VII:
THE END GAME

Chapter 23

Pre-Closing

I like work; it fascinates me,
I can sit and look at it for hours.
~Jerome K. Jerome

      Many things that still need to be done to ensure a smooth transition of ownership to the new buyers. Be sure to check out the closing and moving checklists in the appendix. There you will find valuable step-by-step timelines of tasks that need to be completed to ensure a successful transition. We will discuss the major ones in detail in this chapter.

      Organization is the key to success. If you are using an agent in this transaction, the agent should provide you with all of the necessary steps during the pre-closing phase. If not, I have included them in this chapter.

      For starters, you will most likely need movers to haul contents to your new place. Ideally, this should be scheduled after the home inspection contingencies have been satisfied. However, depending upon the time of year, it may be best to call around ahead of time to get some estimates and reserve a date before they get booked up. You can always postpone the movers later if closing gets delayed.

Utility and Miscellaneous Transfers

You will need to notify your utility companies that you will be transferring service out of your name and into the buyer's name. These may include electricity, natural gas, oil, propane, and water. Hopefully, the buyers are in the process of also contacting the utility companies. Note that we are transferring the service and not disconnecting service on the day of settlement. This typically works best unless your utility providers prefer not to handle it this way.

The one thing we don't want to have happen is the buyers entering the home to do their final walkthrough the day of closing, only to find the electricity and water are shutoff and they can't adequately evaluate the home. This occurred in my early days of transacting real estate and it was not a good situation. It can also lead to settlement delays if the buyer wants to make an issue of it.

Lastly, should the settlement get delayed a day or two, the utilities will be in the buyer's name. If they take issue with this, remind them that the house is now vacant (hopefully) and not much of any utilities will be consumed.

If the house is still occupied, ensure them that the utilities will be used sparingly. If it's delayed too long, you may need to have services transferred back into your name. I don't recommend this because it is more trouble than it is worth, especially if it's only a day or two.

If you have an oil or propane tank and your area allows you compensation for the remaining fuel at closing, you will need to contact the various companies and have them provide you with an official document stating the amount of fuel left over and the dollar amount it is worth on the day of their visit. This information needs to be provided to the closing agent so the seller can get reimbursed for the remaining fuel. Make sure this important task is taken care of. Your agent should be on top of this and remind you.

If you have private trash and recycle collection, you will also want to notify them of your settlement date so they can close out your account and arrange to pick up the containers. Buyers may want to use the same company and have the cans left behind. It is a nice gesture for your agent to reach out to the buyer's agent and see if that is the case.

These little niceties can help should something minor go wrong during the transaction. Buyers appreciate considerate sellers because they too are under a lot of stress. Little acts of kindness can go a long way.

You will also want to contact your Internet service provider, cable supplier and telephone company if you still have a landline. Most people will just transfer the service to another address or close it out altogether if they are moving into a different service area. I find the majority of sellers do not have landlines anymore as they are now reliant on cell phones.

Eventually, you will want to contact your cell phone provider to see if there are cheaper alternatives since you are moving. If you have an alarm system, ask the buyers if they would like to take over your service. If so, it may save you from paying early termination fees. If not, just call the alarm company to cancel or have your service transferred to another address. You may need additional equipment, depending on whether or not you included your current equipment with the sale of the house.

Lastly, you will want to notify the post office and let them know your future address and when you want the mail to transfer. You don't want any bills going unpaid because of a delay in forwarding.

TIP: *Don't forget to remove your garage door remote controls from your vehicles. It's best to place the remotes in a visible area inside the home so the buyers can check them during their walkthrough. Also remember to assemble extra house keys and write down any useful information the buyer might want, such as the code to the outside garage door keypad or information on the homes alarm system.*

Department of Motor Vehicles - DMV

If you are moving out of state, you should contact the department of motor vehicles of the state to which you are moving and find out what is required to register your vehicle(s). Most states will give you 30 days to register. You will also want to contact your auto insurance company about your new address. Hopefully your rates will decrease with the move.

I don't recommend contacting your homeowners insurance company to cancel until the house has closed escrow and you have the settlement check in hand, along with verification that your mortgage has been satisfied. Better to be safe and pay a couple of extra dollars per day to make sure you are officially off the hook. Most likely, you will be using the same company to insure your new property so they will be on top of it. I would rather have policies overlap than have a lapse in coverage. Be sure to check out the helpful *Closing Checklist* located in the Appendix at the back of the book.

In the next chapter, I will cover the holy grail of real estate, which is the closing itself. We have a few things left to go over. You are almost there. Grab a bottle of bubbly and meet me on the next page!

Chapter 24

Closing

"It ain't over, till it's over."
~Yogi Berra

Truer words have never been spoken, especially pertaining to sports and real estate closings. I try not to get too excited until I am leaving the settlement table with a check in hand. Anything and everything can go wrong at the worst possible moment. When it's over, you will not hear plus-sized ladies sing, or angel bells ring, however, it will be a fantastic day!

Final Walkthrough

There are only a few remaining things that need to go smoothly to get to the finish line. The first is the buyer's final walkthrough of the property, where they will be visiting your home one last time before they legally own it. Here is a list of what the buyers be reviewing during the final walkthrough:

1. The house is in the same or better condition than when they wrote the offer.
2. The repairs have been satisfactorily completed.
3. All exclusions have been removed.
4. All inclusions remain in the house.
5. The main heating or air conditioning systems are in working order, depending on the time of year.
6. The plumbing and electrical systems are all working with no noticeable defects or leaks.
7. The interior is broom clean and free of trash.
8. The exterior is in the same condition as before with no trees lying around, and the grass looks the way it did when the offer was written.

I once had a big tree fall in the front yard of a listing client on a Sunday afternoon the day before closing. You never know when Murphy's Law is going to enter into the picture. The buyers discovered it on their walkthrough and demanded that the tree be removed the next day before closing or the deal would be postponed. I made some phone calls to a few of my key contacts and was able to get the tree removed the next morning. Closing took place as scheduled.

While inside, buyers will be checking to make sure everything is still working properly. This final part should be a piece of cake, since you maintained your home nicely during the entire process.

TIP: *Andrew P. Taylor, an attorney with Copeland Taylor, LLC says he, "Sometimes encounters disgruntled buyers at the settlement table with complaints about sellers swapping out inclusions before settlement with* *items of lesser value." He states, "Sellers need to disclose exactly which items will remain with the property and should not be exchanging goods prior to closing without the buyer's knowledge or consent. Doing so can create contentious settlements which can lead to unwanted seller repercussions." He explains, "Sellers should replace wanted inclusions prior to showing the house so buyers don't get too attached to them."*

Sometimes sellers like to be present for the walkthrough to show buyers how things work and to give them a general overview of the home. While this can be a warm and friendly gesture, I have witnessed sellers stay for the final walkthrough and say things they probably shouldn't be saying at this crucial time in the sales process.

For example, I remember sellers being present at a final walkthrough and explaining to the buyers the best way to prevent a basement water leak. This information should have been disclosed in the seller's disclosure. In this case, the buyers needed to close, but if they'd had more flexibility, closing may have been pushed off.

I have also witnessed sellers talk too much about things that don't concern the buyers. For example, some sellers have gone on and on about how much bigger their new home is and that it's closer to the beach, etc. This is surely going to make the buyers feel as if their home purchase is inferior to the seller's new property and it robs them of the joy and satisfaction they should be feeling. If you do stick around for their visit, try not to discuss your next property and focus on the buyers and their terrific new home.

Soon after the walkthrough, I will contact the buyer's agent and ask if everything went all right and if any issues need to be addressed. Typically, if the seller followed the contract and left the inclusions in place, removed the exclusions, left the utilities on for the final walkthrough and had the house broom clean, everything should be fine. If there is an issue, I will contact my seller and let them know and discuss a solution.

The one thing you do not want is to find out there is an issue with the walkthrough at the eleventh hour while at the closing table. This is why I suggest your agent be proactive and inquire about any problems sooner rather than later. It will often be something small, such as they couldn't get some lights to turn on. Many times, these little issues can be resolved over the telephone with simple instructions.

Closing Disclosure - CD

Approximately one day before closing, contact the lender or have your agent call to make sure everything is on track and that the buyers have been *cleared to close.* Then have them contact the closing agent and ask for a copy of the *Closing Disclosure* or CD. This used to be called the *HUD-1* until the name changed sometime after the 2008 recession and new regulations took place. The *Closing Disclosure* will give you a breakdown of all of your expenses, to include: mortgage balance, transfer taxes, commissions, etc. It will also show you your credits or reimbursements, such as sewer taxes, HOA fees, property taxes, etc. The CD will also provide you with the magic number of what your final payout amount will be, aka the settlement check!

Look over the CD carefully and make sure the numbers are similar to what you were expecting. Bring that same copy with you to compare with what they provide you at the actual closing to make sure the numbers are the same. If not, you will easily be able to see where any discrepancies are.

Don't be alarmed if it's not exactly the same. Occasionally expenses such as the final water bill get overlooked and have to be added on the day of closing. Sometimes the error will be on the buyer's side and the amount you receive will be slightly higher. In any case, just make sure that the change makes sense. If not, ask for clarification to get a better understanding of the charge. Perhaps you have previously paid the amount in question? If so, this should be brought to their attention.

Money can be set aside and paid later if need be. Don't be intimidated to speak up. If you prefer not to, let your agent know about the issue so he or she can go to bat for you. Best to get it right!

TIP: *It's a good idea to bring copies of utility payment information with you to the settlement table so you can verify a payment if needed. Better to have more information and not need it than to need it and not have it.*

On the morning of settlement, contact the lender or have your agent call to make sure the funds will be at settlement as planned. Also call the closing agent's office on the day of closing to make sure the funds have arrived.

There's not much you can do if the lender's money doesn't show up.

Some closing agents will have you sign the paperwork ahead of time in what is termed a *dry closing*, with no keys or checks being dispersed until the money makes its appearance via a wire transfer. Once the money has arrived, the buyer can pick up the keys and the seller will get their proceeds. This saves everyone from having to reconvene later to sign all of the documents.

Closing Location

The closing itself will be held at either the attorney's office or the title company's office, whoever is required to conduct the closing. Some states are *attorney states*, which means attorneys are required to settle the transaction. In other states, this is not the case and title companies will settle it.

It is always a good sign if the buyer's loan officer attends the settlement, since they will know how to push the right buttons should the money get tied up. I have never had a settlement not go through when the buyer's loan officer has attended the closing.

Typically, buyers and sellers are meeting for the first time and they all may be nervous. You will have plenty of time to converse with one another during the closing process. Take my advice and make your first meeting at the settlement table.

If you want to impress your buyers for the walkthrough, leave them a nice bottle of champagne or sparkling cider in the refrigerator with a note of congratulations and how much you enjoyed and will miss your home. This a very nice gesture that will carry over to the settlement table and provide for wonderful conversation.

Meeting the Buyers

Typically, when buyers and sellers meet for the first time at the closing office, it should be very cordial, with compliments being passed between the parties. The group will then be escorted to a conference room where the closing will commence. The attorney or title agent will usually ask the buyer how the walkthrough went and if there are any issues, and he will ask for legal identification from both parties.

While at the settlement table, it may be suggested that you provide the buyers with your contact information. Although it is a very nice gesture, it is not a good idea to give buyers your personal information because it can lead to a string of phone calls regarding possible issues with the home and thus a never-ending transaction.

Most contracts state that buyers are not buying new construction and issues are bound to arise, so it's not surprising when something goes wrong with a pre-owned property. If you hired a real estate professional to coordinate your sale, they should also be willing to handle any post-closing phone calls and be your mediator should something arise.

Don't forget, home warranties can avert many of these phone calls because any issues with the home will be directed to the home warranty company. This takes the sellers and their agent out of the firing line. Home warranties make a wonderful inclusion when selling your home because the warranty company gets the repair calls and not the seller.

At the settlement table, separate closing disclosures are distributed to the buyers and sellers. For privacy reasons, each has their own CD, since information such as the amount of proceeds the seller will be receiving is considered confidential information. The closing agent will first discuss the figures with the buyers to make sure everything looks good. Then the seller will review their CD with the closing agent to ensure all of the figures are accurate.

Since both agents were proactive in getting their clients a copy of the CD ahead of time, both parties should be satisfied and ready to sign the documents. There will be approximately 8-10 copies of CD's signed by both parties, because lenders, attorneys and real estate brokers all want original documents with signatures.

Once all documents are fully executed, the seller will hand over any remaining keys and instructions to the new owners and any final questions will be answered. If the seller is lucky, the closing agent will let them leave with a check before the buyer signs all of their loan documents. If the buyer's lender requires the closing agent to email copies of the signed documents for approval, the seller will have to wait until the end of the closing in case something else needs to be signed.

When the contracts have been blessed by the lender, the settlement agent will announce that the documents have been approved and they can now disperse the checks to the seller and agents. Sometimes even the buyer will receive a small check due to an overpayment with the lender. Once everyone has received their checks, the parties will shake hands and exit the room. Closing is now official! It is safe to pop the champagne corks and celebrate!

Taxes

Sorry to rain on your parade, but it's important to know where you stand regarding taxes. How well you did with your sales proceeds will determine if you will be owing Uncle Sam any taxes on the sale. Richard Miller, CPA, PFS, with Van Buren Financial Group, LLC says, "The question I always get is how long will the government give me to reinvest the proceeds of the sale of my home into a new principal residence so I won't pay any taxes." The answer to that question is: "The rule changed in 1997 and there is no way to avoid paying taxes on the gain of a personal residence that exceeds $250,000 single filer and $500,000 for married filing joint. There are complicated rules you must follow to receive the $250,000 and $500,000 tax-free gain from the sale of your personal residence."

He states, "there are three tests that you must pass: the *ownership test*, the *use test* and the *one sale in two years test*. I recommend that you see a tax advisor prior to entering into an agreement of sale. You need to make sure your particular situation qualifies for the exclusion." His tips are as follows:

> ➤ Keep all the documents related to the purchase of your home.
> ➤ Keep all the receipts for your home improvements.
> ➤ Keep all the documents related to the sale of your home.
> ➤ Keep track of all energy credits claimed on the property.

In the final chapter, I will reflect on the selling process and review some final thoughts. Grab a celebratory drink along with a fake cigar and meet me on the next page for the conclusion!

Chapter 25

Conclusion

"Always believe something wonderful is going to happen. Even with all the ups and downs, never take a day for granted. Smile, cherish the little things and remember to hug the ones you really love."
~Charles M. Shulz

Congratulations on making it to the final chapter! Hopefully, you have gained some valuable insight and newfound wisdom after reading about my decades of experience in real estate.

You've done your homework, purged your possessions, made necessary repairs and cleaned your home like it's never been cleaned before. You decided whether to go it alone or hire a competent real estate agent to represent you. You chose a listing price, filled out umpteen pages of seller's disclosures and allowed buyers to visit your home at all hours of the day. You successfully negotiated a purchase agreement and allowed inspectors to poke and prod your beloved home. You successfully negotiated a repair addendum, helped coordinate home repairs and maintained the home's beauty so the appraiser could come inside and properly evaluate your property. You contacted the utility companies to transfer your service and closed out any other accounts such as trash removal and Internet service. You also contacted a moving company and arranged for all of your remaining possessions to be moved. Finally, you left nothing to chance by preparing the home for the final walkthrough.

You did all of this while keeping the home looking its best in the face of having to move out. You deserve a BIG PAT on the BACK! What you have accomplished is considered the second hardest, most stressful thing that we humans endure (the first being the loss of a loved one). Be thankful that it wasn't the latter.

As you have probably discovered, moving is not easy, and neither is selling a home. There are many challenging hurdles that must be overcome in order to get to the finish line. Some agents compare selling a home to piloting a plane in rough weather. There are periods of calm followed by episodes of turbulence, rain showers and the occasional white-knuckle moments when you are not sure if you are going to make it. However, with the right training and experience, you and your co-pilot will be able to land the deal successfully.

Throughout this book, I have given you my candid opinion regarding the sales process, buyers, real estate agents, inspectors, appraisers and everything in between. I have provided you with firsthand accounts and experiences that have shaped me into a seasoned professional.

Real estate agents and Realtors® do not learn how to navigate this business merely by obtaining their licenses. Real expertise is only learned in the trenches by being faced with real situations and learning how to deal with them. It involves sidestepping the pitfalls and recognizing what you don't know or that to which you have ever given thought. You now have a more thorough understanding of the sales process than most newer agents. Real estate courses and exams deal more with rules and regulations than they do the ins and outs of the actual selling process.

I've read other real estate books where the author will lead you to believe selling your home is simple and that anyone with little to no experience can easily pull off a successful transaction. While this is possible given the ideal situation, I just don't think it is practical advice. There are too many things that can and do go wrong when selling real estate. Being a naïve seller is just going to make matters worse. As I have said before, knowledge is power, and the more of it you have, the better off you will be.

Thank you for taking this real estate journey with me. I hope you enjoyed it as much as I enjoyed writing it and reliving the many memories (at least most of them!).

I wish you good luck in all of your future real estate dealings. Please visit my website *www.realestatedave1.com* and send me a note letting me know how you did with your home sale. If you are going to be purchasing a property, look for my next book titled: <u>Expert 21st Century Advice on BUYING your Next Home for Maximum Value</u>, currently in production. Best Wishes,

Real Estate Dave

Appendix

Glossary of Terms:

Agency - The relationship between a principal and an agent wherein the agent is authorized to represent the principal in certain transactions.

Agent – One who acts or has the power to act for another. A fiduciary relationship is created under the law of agency when a property owner, as the principal, executes a listing agreement authorizing a licensed real estate broker to be his or her agent. A prospective buyer may authorize a real estate broker to act as the buyer's agent to find a property

Antitrust Laws – Laws designed to preserve the free enterprise of the open marketplace by making illegal certain private conspiracies to minimize competition.

Appraisal – An estimate of the value of something. An opinion of a property's market value with detailed market information.

Appraiser – Licensed and certified to provide an unbiased estimate of value in real estate.

Asbestos – A mineral once used in insulation and other materials that have been deemed hazardous.

Broker – A broker is required to have a broker's license that enables them to own a real estate firm and hire real estate agents.

Real estate Brokerage – The bringing together of parties interested in making a real estate transaction.

Buyer's Agent – A real estate professional who is under contract to locate a property for a buyer and represent the buyer's interests in a transaction.

Buyer's Broker – Residential real estate brokers and their agents who represent prospective buyers exclusively.

Buyer Agency Agreement – A written agreement signed by a prospective buyer to have their interests represented by a real estate broker.

Closing Statement – A detailed cash accounting of a real estate transaction showing all cash received, all charges and credits made and all cash paid out in the transaction.

Code of Ethics – A written system of standards for ethical conduct.

Commission – Payment to a real estate professional for services rendered, such as in the sale or purchase of real property, which is usually a percentage of the selling price.

Competitive Market Analysis (CMA) – A comparison of the prices of recently sold homes that are similar to a seller's home in terms of location, style, and amenities.

Condominium - The absolute ownership of a unit in a multi-unit building based on a legal description of the space the unit occupies, plus an undivided interest in the ownership of common elements within the building or development that are owned jointly with other condo unit owners.

Contingency – Provisions in a contract that require a certain act to be done or a certain event to occur before the contract becomes binding.

Contract – A legally enforceable promise must be performed and for which, if a breach of the promise occurs, the law provides a legal remedy.

Conventional Loan – A loan that requires no federally sponsored insurance or guarantee.

Cooperating Broker – The broker who participates in facilitating a real estate transaction along with the broker who listed the property.

Counteroffer – A new offer made in response to an offer received.

Credit – On a closing statement (CD), an amount entered in a person's favor.

Debit – On a closing statement (CD), an amount charged; an amount the debited party must pay.

Deed – A written instrument which conveys title to or an interest in real estate.

Default – The nonperformance of a duty, whether arising under a contract or otherwise; failure to meet an obligation when due.

Depreciation – In an appraisal, a loss of value in property due to any cause.

Designated Agent – A real estate professional authorized by a broker to act as the agent for a specific principal in a real estate transaction.

Dual Agency – Representing both parties to a transaction.

Earnest Money – Money deposited by a buyer under the terms of a contract, to be forfeited if the buyer defaults.

Employee – Someone who works as a direct employee for an employer and for tax purposes has employee status.

Encapsulation – A method of controlling environmental contamination by sealing off a dangerous substance, such as asbestos.

Escrow – The closing of a transaction through a third party called an escrow agent, who receives certain funds and documents to be delivered upon the performance of conditions outlined in the escrow instructions.

Escrow Account – A financial instrument whereby an asset or escrow money is held by a third party on behalf of two other parties in the process of a transaction.

Estate – all the money and property owned by a particular person, especially at death.

Exclusive Right to Sell Listing – A listing contract under which the owner appoints a real estate professional as his exclusive agent for a designated period of time to sell a specified property and agrees to pay the real estate professional a commission when the property is sold, whether by the real estate professional or another real estate professional.

Executed Contract – A written contract that has been signed by both parties.

Execution Date – The date when the last party signs a written contract, thus executing it.

Fannie Mae – A government-supervised enterprise established to purchase any kind of mortgage loans in the secondary mortgage market from the primary lender.

Federal Home Loan Mortgage Corp (Freddie Mac) – A government-supervised enterprise established to purchase primarily conventional mortgage loans in the secondary mortgage market.

Federal Housing Administration (FHA) – A United States government agency that sets standards for construction and underwriting and insures loans made by banks and other private lenders for real estate.

Fee Simple – The highest interest in real estate recognized by law; the holder is entitled to all rights to the property.

Fiduciary – One in whom trust and confidence are placed; a reference to a real estate professional employed under the terms of the listing agreement.

FHA Loan – A loan insured by the Federal Housing Administration and made by an approved lender in accordance with FHA regulations.

Foreclosure – A legal procedure whereby property used as security for a debt is sold to satisfy the debt in the event of default in payment of the mortgage note or default of other terms in the mortgage document.

Freddie Mac – *See* Federal Home Loan Mortgage Corp

Functional Obsolescence – A loss of value to an improvement of real estate arising from problems of design or utility.

General Lien – The right of a creditor to have all of a debtor's property, both real and personal, sold to satisfy a debt.

Ginnie Mae – A government agency that plays an important role in the secondary mortgage market. It guarantees mortgage-backed securities using FHA-insured and VA guaranteed loans as collateral.

Grantee – A person who receives a transfer of real property from a grantor.

Grantor – The owner transferring title to, or an interest in real property to a grantee.

Heir – One who may inherit or succeed to an interest in property under the state law of descent when the owner dies without leaving a valid will.

Home Equity Loan – A loan under which a property owner uses the property as collateral and can draw funds up to a prearranged amount against the property.

Homeowners Insurance – Insurance that covers a residential real estate owner against loss from fire, theft, weather, liability, and other risks.

Improvement – Any structure erected on a site to enhance the value of the property.

Income Approach – The process of estimating the value of an income-producing property through capitalization of the annual net income expected to be produced by the property during its remaining useful life.

Independent Contractor – Someone who is retained to perform a certain role and is subject to direction of another only to the end result and not as to the way in which the act is performed.

Investment – Money directed toward the purchase, improvement, and development of an asset in expectation of income or profits.

Judgment – The formal decision of a court upon the respective rights and claims of the parties to an action or suit. After a judgment has been entered and recorded with the county recorder, it usually becomes a general lien on the property of the defendant.

Lead Paint – Used as a pigment and drying agent in alkyd oil-based paint. A known health hazard that may or may not have been used in homes prior to 1979.

Lease – A contract between a landlord and a tenant that transfers the right to exclusive possession and use of the landlord's real property.

License – In real estate practice, the privilege or right granted to a person by a state to operate as a real estate broker or salesperson.

Lien – A right given by law to certain creditors to have their debts paid out of the property of a defaulting debtor, usually by means of a court sale.

Listing Broker – The broker from whose office a listing agreement is initiated.

Market Value – The most probable price that a property would bring in an arm's length transaction under normal market conditions.

Mechanics Lien – A statutory lien created in favor of contractors, laborers, material supplies and others who have performed work or furnished materials in the erection or repair of a building.

Minor – A person who has not reached the age of majority and does not have the legal capacity to transfer title to real property.

Mortgage – A conditional pledge of real estate as security for the payment of a debt.

Mortgage Broker – An agent of a lender who brings the lender and borrower together. The broker receives compensation for this service.

Mortgage Insurance Premium (MIP) – The FHA insurance that is a percentage of the loan amount in which the borrower is charged as a premium.

Multiple Listing Service (MLS) – An organization composed of member real estate professionals who agree to share their listing agreements with one another in the hope of procuring buyers. MLS accepts listings from their member real estate professionals.

National Association of Realtors® (NAR) – The largest real estate organization in the world. NAR members subscribe to a strict code of ethics.

Note – A financial instrument in which a borrower promises to repay their debt obligation.

Open Listing – A listing contract under which the real estate professional's compensation is contingent on the real estate professional producing a ready and able buyer before the property is sold by the seller or another real estate professional.

Percolation Test – A test of soil to determine whether it will absorb and drain water adequately to use a septic system for sewage disposal.

Personal Property - is movable property. In common law systems, personal property may also be called chattels. In civil law systems, personal property is often called movable property or movables, any property that can be moved from one location to another.

Power of Attorney – A written instrument authorizing a person, the attorney-in-fact, to act as agent for another person to the extent indicated in the instrument.

Prepaid Items – Items on a closing statement that have been paid in advance either by a buyer or seller in a real estate transaction.

Price Fixing – *See* Antitrust Laws

Principal – A sum loaned or employed as a fund or an investment, as distinguished from its income or profits. The main party to a transaction – the person for whom the agent works.

Private Mortgage Insurance (PMI) – Insurance provided by a private carrier that protects a lender against a loss in the event of a deficiency or foreclosure.

Probate – A legal process by which a court determines who will inherit a decedent's property and what the estate's assets are.

Promissory Note – A financing instrument that states the terms of the underlying obligation and is signed by its maker.

Prorations – Expenses, either prepaid or paid in arrears, that are divided or distributed between the buyer and the seller at the closing.

Radon – A naturally-occurring, colorless, odorless, tasteless noble gas caused by decaying radium in the ground. It is suspected of causing lung cancer.

Real Estate – Land, a portion of the earth's surface extending downward to the center of the earth and upward into space, including all things permanently attached to it whether naturally or artificially.

Real Estate Agent/Licensee - In real estate practice, a person who has the skills and knowledge to be licensed as a real estate broker or salesperson.

Real Estate License Law

Real Property - The interests, benefits, and rights inherent in real estate ownership; often used as a synonym for real estate.

REALTOR® - A registered trademarked term reserved for the sole use of active members of state and local REALTOR® associations affiliated with the National Association of Realtors®.

Recording - The act of entering or recording documents affecting or conveying interests in real estate in the recorder's office established in each county.

Rent - A fixed periodic payment made by a tenant of a property to the owner for the possession and use, usually by prior agreement of the parties.

Sales Associate - A person who performs real estate activities while employed by a licensed real estate broker.

Sales Comparison Approach - The process of estimating the value of real property by examining and comparing sales and listings of comparable properties.

Satisfaction of Mortgage - A document acknowledging the payment of mortgage debt along with release or discharge when a note has been fully paid.

Security Deposit - A payment by a tenant, held by the landlord during the lease term and kept on default or on the destruction of the premises by the tenant.

Sellers Agent - An agent who represents only the seller in a real estate transaction.

Sellers Disclosure - Documents completed by the seller of a home, listing any known issues of the property, including home improvements.

Septic System - A septic system is an efficient, self-contained, underground wastewater treatment system.

Short Sale – Sale of real estate in which the sales price is less than the remaining indebtedness owed by the seller.

Special Agent – One who is authorized by a principal to perform a single act or transaction.

Statute of Frauds – The part of a state law that requires certain instruments, such as deeds, real estate sales, contracts and certain leases to be in writing in order to be legally enforceable.

Subagent – A cooperating agent working with the broker on behalf of the broker's client.

Subdivision – A tract of land divided by the owner into blocks, building lots and streets according to a recorded subdivision plat.

Supply and Demand – The appraisal principle that follows the interrelationship of the supply and demand for real estate.

Survey – The process by which boundaries are measured and land areas are determined; the on-site measurement of lot lines, dimensions and position of the house on a lot, including the determination of any existing encroachments.

Tenant – One who holds or possesses lands or tenements by any kind of right or title.

Time is of the Essence – A phrase in a contract that requires the performance of a certain act within a stated period of time.

Title – The right to ownership, or the ownership of land. The evidence of ownership of land.

Title Insurance – A policy insuring a property owner or mortgagee against loss by reason of defects in the title to a parcel of real estate, other than encumbrances, defects and matters specifically excluded by the policy.

Title Search – The examination of public records relating to real estate to determine the current state of ownership along with property liens.

Transfer Tax – Tax stamps required to be affixed to a deed by state and or local laws. Payment of tax when a property is transferred via purchase and sale.

Trust – A fiduciary arrangement whereby property is conveyed to a person or institution, called a trustee, to be held and administered on behalf of another person, called a beneficiary.

Trust Deed – An instrument used to create a mortgage lien by which the borrower conveys title to a trustee, who holds it as security for the benefit of the note holder. Also called a deed of trust.

Trustee – One who is entrusted and holds legal title to a property and administers the property for the benefit of a beneficiary.

Trustor – A borrower in a deed of trust loan transaction; one who places a property in a trust. Also termed grantor.

USDA Loan – Also known as the USDA Rural Development Guaranteed Housing Loan Program, is a mortgage loan offered to rural property owners in specific areas by the U.S. Department of Agriculture (USDA).

U.S. Department of Housing and Administration (HUD) - Government agency that administers the Fair Housing Act to ensure fair housing in the marketplace. Ginnie Mae is a division of HUD.

VA Loan – The U.S. Department of Veterans Affairs (VA) is authorized to guarantee loans used to purchase or construct homes for eligible veterans and their spouses.

Well – An excavation or structure created in the ground by digging or drilling to access liquid resources, typically water.

Will – A written document, properly witnessed, providing for the transfer of title to property owned by the deceased, called the testator.

For-Sale Checklist

This checklist will ensure you are ready to show your home to the public. It is applicable with or without using an agent.

Documents

- ☐ Listing Packet with photos
- ☐ Sellers Disclosures filled out
- ☐ Property Description sheet with room measurements
- ☐ List of home improvements and date of completion
- ☐ Warranty information for repairs and improvements
- ☐ Copy of Deed Restrictions
- ☐ Monthly Utility Costs

To Be Completed

- ☐ For Sale Sign put in the yard
- ☐ House listed with the MLS* and/or online websites
- ☐ Lockbox* installed on the door and extra key made
- ☐ Plan for your pets during showings
- ☐ Lock away important documents, jewelry, and meds
- ☐ Review appointment procedures and showing availability*
- ☐ Inside the house is clean, neat and well organized
- ☐ Outside the lawn is cut, trimmed and neat
- ☐ All photos have been taken

<u>Ongoing</u>

- ☐ Obtain feedback
- ☐ Address feedback issues
- ☐ Inside and outside of the house are kept immaculate
- ☐ Brochures and disclosures are replenished
- ☐ Schedule an Open House
- ☐ Review safety procedures

* If using a real estate agent.

Open House Checklist

This checklist is to ensure you have everything ready for an open house. It is applicable with or without a real estate agent.

7 Days Before Open House

- ☐ Include all documents described in Listing Checklist
- ☐ Install *Open Sunday Sign*
- ☐ Input *Open House* in local print publications
- ☐ Input *Open House* into to MLS*
- ☐ Input *Open House* on third-party real estate websites

1 Day Before Open House

- ☐ Get permission from neighbors and install directional signs at several cross streets
- ☐ Thoroughly clean house so it is neat and organized
- ☐ Cut grass and trim yard
- ☐ Safely store important documents, jewelry, and medicines
- ☐ Prepare a sign-in sheet
- ☐ Purchase some bottled water and snacks with minimal crumbs that won't stain furniture
- ☐ Make plans for children and pets

Day of Open House

- ☐ Install balloons on the open house sign
- ☐ Check directional signs and add balloons

- ☐ Organize listing materials
- ☐ Display sign-in sheet and include a pen or pencil
- ☐ Set out bottled water and snacks with a *Help Yourself* note
- ☐ Set out napkins
- ☐ Turn off the television and other distractions
- ☐ Make arrangements for your children and pets
- ☐ Turn on all lights including basement and garage
- ☐ Set thermostat to a comfortable temperature
- ☐ Review safety procedures

* If using a real estate agent.

Moving Timeline

This document will help you organize all of your tasks starting six weeks away from the closing date.

6 Weeks Before Move

- ☐ Create an inventory sheet of items to be moved
- ☐ Get quotes from moving companies
- ☐ Discard or donate any unwanted items
- ☐ Gather packing tape, boxes or plastic bins, markers and other packing materials
- ☐ Notify insurance companies for new estimates on home and auto
- ☐ Seek employer benefits if the move is work related
- ☐ Contact new schools and verify enrollment

4 Weeks Before Move

- ☐ Contact utility companies for transfer of ownership or cancellation of service
- ☐ Notify utility companies of your new address
- ☐ Ask for a copy of medical records from doctors and specialists
- ☐ Prepare mower and other small engine equipment for your move (drain fuel, oil, etc.)
- ☐ Return borrowed items such as library books, videos, etc.
- ☐ Contact former and new Department of Motor Vehicles if moving out of state

☐ Box up your items to be moved and label each box with a number and proper room placement

☐ Count the total number of boxes and create an inventory checklist

1 Week Before Move

☐ Plan closing day itinerary and make plans for kids and pets

☐ Notify U.S. Post Office for the upcoming change of address

☐ Notify banks of change of address, close any unwanted accounts and transfer funds

☐ Finalize remaining items for packing

☐ Disassemble any furniture (cribs, large tables) too large to move through doorways

☐ Notify and cancel any remaining services for newspaper, cable, phone, internet and lawn care

☐ Review the condition of your furniture for scratches and blemishes prior to the move, or take photos

☐ Label where furniture goes in the new house

Moving Day

☐ Last-minute walkthrough of current house for any remaining items

☐ Check closets, dishwasher, washing machine and clothes dryer for any remaining items

☐ Scan walls for pictures, paintings, and mirrors

☐ Check all cabinets, drawers and underneath sinks

☐ Leave extra keys and garage door remote controls visible in the house

☐ Lock all doors and windows

New Home Check-In

☐ Label each room for proper placement of boxes
☐ Compare incoming boxes to inventory checklist
☐ Review furniture and box contents for damage
☐ Check moving truck for leftover items
☐ Sign moving company receipt to confirm shipment

Closing Checklist

This checklist covers the timeline between offer acceptance and the closing date. It is applicable with or without a real estate agent.

Offer Acceptance

- ☐ Agreement of Sale signed along with seller's disclosures
- ☐ Earnest money deposit received and placed in escrow
- ☐ Appointment center is notified of contract and showings are canceled per seller's request*
- ☐ MLS is notified of contract and status is amended*
- ☐ Notify closing agent (attorney, title company) and provide with all sales documents
- ☐ Buyer applies for a mortgage and forwards their documents to the lender
- ☐ Home inspections ordered by the buyer and inspection dates are provided to the seller

Within Two Weeks after Acceptance

- ☐ Have a plan for children and pets during inspections
- ☐ Home inspections conducted and completed
- ☐ Inspection reports and buyer's request for repairs are submitted to the seller
- ☐ Seller reviews report and asks pertinent questions
- ☐ Seller written response to buyers request for repairs
- ☐ Buyer and seller negotiate and finalize a request for repairs agreement
- ☐ Closing agent orders title search

☐ Inside the house remains clean, neat and organized

☐ The outside lawn is cut, trimmed and neat

Three to Four Weeks after Acceptance

☐ Seller makes appointments with local contractors

☐ Seller receives work estimates and finalizes paperwork with contractors

☐ Work begins on the property

☐ The appraisal is ordered by the lender

☐ Seller contacts utility companies about the transfer of service

☐ Inside and outside of the house are kept immaculate

Two to Three Weeks Prior to Closing

☐ Appraisal results are provided to buyers with any problems reported to sellers

☐ Mortgage commit is received and reviewed for lender conditions

☐ Contact closing agent for time and place of settlement

☐ Buyers schedule their final walkthrough

Week of Closing

☐ Remaining heating fuel (oil, propane, etc.) is measured with estimated value sent to the closing agent for seller reimbursement**

☐ Water meter is read by water company for transfer of service

☐ Home repairs are finalized and paid for by the seller

☐ Buyer receives a copy of repair receipts and warranty info

☐ Yard sign is removed from property

☐ Final walkthrough completed by buyers

☐ Any local government inspections need to be completed and approved

☐ Buyer is given the *clear to close* from their lender

☐ The closing agent provides closing disclosures (CD) for advance review

Closing Day

☐ Lender wires funds, and sends closing documents to closing agent's office

☐ Buyer, sellers, closing agent and real estate agents assemble at the closing agent's office

☐ Buyers and sellers sign all applicable transaction documents

☐ Earnest money check is provided to the closing agent

☐ Buyers sign all lender documents

☐ Seller provides the buyer with additional keys

☐ Bank approves signed documents

☐ Seller is presented with sales check and Buyer is presented with the signed deed

☐ The closing is final!

*If using a real estate agent.

**If seller is reimbursed for heating fuel in your area.

Index

C

D

doors, 45
downsizing, 23
downspouts, 42
drain field, 55
drinking water, 53
driveway, 42, 156, 164, 184, 233
dryer hose, 139
dryers, 40
drywall, 47
dual agency, 269
DuPont employees, 121

E

earnest money, 208, 213, 269
effervescence, 230
EIFS, see stucco
electrical, 48, 139, 149, 231, 249, 255
electrician, 48, 231
electricity, 48, 249
electronic safety lasers, 139
electronic surveillance equipment, 149
EMD: See earnest money
employee, 269
encapsulate, 50, 269
endorsement to the agreement of Sale, 231
entertainment system, 193, 198
Equifax, 211
escrow, 77, 269
account, 269
funds, 77
Estate, 2-3, 5, 13, 83-85, 95, 102-103, 113, 203, 266, 269, 274
exclusions, 255, 257
exclusive right to sell listing, 269
executed contract, 269
execution date, 270
Experian, 211
exterior, 4, 29, 41

F

fair housing laws, 74
family room, 3, 29, 40
Fannie Mae, 270
Federal Housing Administration, 45, 65, 216-221, 242, 270, 272
fee appraisal, 123, 125-126
fee simple, 270
feedback, 63, 173-175, 181, 184, 278

I

J

K

L

M

magic erasers, 31
market value, 272
marketing, 4, 6, 83, 92, 107, 155, 161, 164, 202
    materials, 107, 164, 202
    your home, 6, 155
master bedroom, 28, 38-39, 168
maximum profit, 34, 56, 78, 149, 163, 200, 204
mechanics lien, 272
medications, 146, 173
Miller, Richard, 261
Minwax, 32
MIP, see mortgage insurance
missing steps, 148
MLS, see multiple listing service
model homes, 165
mold, 37, 56, 139, 185
mortgage, 17, 43, 76-77, 179, 210, 216, 218, 220, 223, 240, 251, 257, 270, 272, 274, 276, 284-285
mortgage broker, 272
mortgage insurance, 218, 221, 272
Movement Mortgage, 44, 211
movie passes, 204
moving, 7, 15, 17, 22, 24-26, 33, 35, 66, 91, 136, 156, 241, 248, 250-251, 265, 281, 283
moving trucks, 15, 17
mulch, 42
multiple listing service, 71, 90, 92, 102-103, 124, 155, 159-160, 164, 174, 181, 213, 272, 277, 279, 284
municipalities, 235
Murphy's Oil Soap, 32

N

naïve seller, 266
NAR, 84, 272, 274
National Association of Realtors®, 84, 272, 274
natural gas, 249
natural light, 185
neighborhood, 67, 69, 126, 198, 200
neighbors, 156, 179, 197, 199, 279
nerdwallet.com, 7
news print, 93, 155, 157, 282
note, 3, 249, 272-273

O

P

T

Y

Z

About the Author

Dave's fascination with real estate began in 1997 after first being introduced to the field while actively selling his first home. He became a Realtor® in 1998 and received his broker's license in 2008. Licensed in Delaware and Pennsylvania he has sold hundreds of homes and continues to prosper as a Realtor® and real estate investor. He is a graduate of the University of Delaware and currently resides in Wilmington, Delaware.

He has held many leadership positions in the industry including, Treasurer of the New Castle County Board of Realtors®, (NCCBOR). Executive Committee Member, NCCBOR. Member of the Board of Directors, Delaware Association of Realtors®, (DAR). Member of the Professional Standards Committee, NCCBOR.

In his spare time, he's managed to achieve the Distinguished Toastmaster Award (DTM public speaking) with Toastmasters International and has served in various leadership roles within the organization.

He has graciously volunteered his efforts with various organizations including, The DuPont Children's Hospital, Habitat for Humanity, and Meals on Wheels. He currently serves as a Worship Associate at his local church.

Made in USA - Kendallville, IN
1120041_9781734748208
06.05.2020 0747